THE

UNDYING

FLAME

Mariano Moreno of
Buenos Aires

THE UNDYING FLAME

Mariano Moreno of Buenos Aires

by

ELLEN GARWOOD

AMERICAN STUDIES CENTER
WASHINGTON, D.C.
and
FUNDACIÓN CARLOS PELLEGRINI
BUENOS AIRES
1986

Upon Moreno's burial at sea, March 3rd, 1811,
Colonel Cornelio de Saavedra said of him:

"It took so much water to quench so much fire."

And the twentieth-century poet Cupertino del Campo
wrote,

*"So much fire—notwithstanding the
eloquent exclamation of another—not even the
fathomless waters of the sea could extinguish."*

ISBN 0-931727-01-4
Library of Congress Catalog Card No. 85-737-17

THE AMERICAN STUDIES CENTER
426 C Street, N.E.
Washington, D.C. 20002
(202) 547-9409

In memory of my son
Wilmer St. John Garwood, Jr.

Contents

Foreword
by Dr. Mariano J. Drago

The great men of South American independence are practically unknown in Europe. With the exception of Miranda, Bolívar and San Martín, about whom there is only superficial knowledge, little or nothing is known in the Old World of other great figures, both military and civilian, whose thought and action in the movement for independence of Spanish America have written their names large. I call to mind Marshal Sucre, Paez, General O'Higgins, Belgrano, Güemes, Moreno, Rivadavia, Monteagudo, to name only those who have achieved greatest renown. In the United States, on the other hand, there has been noticeable in historical studies, for some time, a growing interest in the sister nations of the continent, particularly Argentina.

Proof of that interest, so gratifying to the Argentines, is the present book which the author, Mrs. Ellen Garwood, has aptly called, *The Undying Flame, Mariano Moreno of Buenos Aires*. It is one of the most complete biographies that I know of the famous Secretary of the Junta of Government of the Provinces of the Río de la Plata. Mrs. Garwood has made an assiduous investigation and study of the most authoritative sources. North American, free of any prejudice of party, her work is the impartial account of the

life of this great man and of the events leading up to the
Argentine Revolution until the death of Moreno in March,
1811.

The author narrates with candor and literary grace
the life of Moreno from infancy, the years of schooling in
Buenos Aires and Chuquisaca, in whose University he
graduated as Doctor in both Laws (Canonical and Civil),
his marriage and return to his native city. She recounts
the first triumphs of the young lawyer—the most important, his defense of freedom of trade before the Consulate
of Buenos Aires, in the famous *Representación de los
Hacendados*, in which there vibrates already the revolutionary accent. She relates in detail his intelligent and
energertic activity in the *Junta de Gobierno*, his work as
newspaper editor, his differences with the President of the
Junta, Colonel Saavedra, and finally the resignation of Moreno—sent by the *Junta* to the Court of Río de Janeiro and
to England on a diplomatic mission which was in reality an
exile—and his death on the high seas.

When he was named Secretary of the *Junta*, Moreno
had not yet completed his thirty-second year. As to character, talent, and culture, he is, by far, the most outstanding
figure of the first patriot government. He was in charge of
the Departments of War and Government which embraced,
at that time, and for years afterwards, foreign relations. In
the short time from the end of May to the first days of
December, 1810, he accomplished the work of administrator
and statesman.

He founded the Public Library and *Gaceta* of Buenos
Aires. "From the heights of his creative thinking and activity," writes the historian, Vicente F. López, "he could descend
to the practical, to the useful, and to the vital needs of
hygiene. Thus it was that he founded a permanent establishment for the propagation of vaccine. He ordered the

repair and leveling of the streets and sidewalks of the city and organized police patrols to assure order in the vicinity."

Of the writers and philosophers of the eighteenth century, Rousseau and his Italian disciple, Filangieri, are those who most influenced Moreno's political thought. He does not appear to have read Montesquieu. Censorship had its reasons for preventing entrance into the colonies of the works of the immortal philosopher who had written in 1748 in *L'Esprit des Lois* this surprising prophecy: "The Indies are the principal; Spain is no more than the accessory. It is in vain that politics wish to subordinate the principal to the accessory."

"The populace ought not to rest content," wrote Moreno in the *Gaceta* of November 1, 1810, "with asking no more of the government than that their leaders work well: It ought to aspire to their never working harm; to their passions having a firmer check than that of their own virtue; to the ideal whereby, marking out the road of their operations by rules incapable of being overturned, the excellence of the government is derived not from the persons who run it but from a firm constitution which obliges the successors to be equally as good as the first, without in any way permitting the first the freedom of doing evil with impunity."

That devotion to the law, that blind faith in its efficacy, are of Rousseaunian inspiration. It is the opposite of Montesquieu, who realistically affirms: "Once corrupted the motives of government, the best laws become bad ones and are turned against the state. When the motives are sound, the bad laws have the same effect as the good: the motive controls the whole."

The Argentine Revolution, like that of Caracas which preceded it, was made under the disguise of loyalty to Ferdinand VII, who, held captive in Valencay, had been one of

the first in congratulating King Joseph. The oath of obedience deceived no one. The Council of Regency, installed on
the Island of Leon, treated as rebels the Spanish colonies
which had set up _Juntas,_ and in Buenos Aires the Cabildo
and the Court refused to respect the authority of the _Junta,_
demanding from it recognition of the Council of Regency.
The _Junta,_ with decision, detained the ex-Viceroy Cisneros
and other Spanish officials who were sent out of the country
on an English ship which set sail June 22, before one month
of the revolution had passed by.

Moreno, from the columns of the _Gaceta,_ was the doc-
trinarian of the revolution and the first to discard the "mask
of Ferdinand" in a series of articles on the objectives of the
Congress called by the _Junta,_ in which he expressed, clearly
and eloquently, the right of the colonies to freedom while,
at the same time, urging that the new state be given a
constitution.

"We have no constitution and without one our hope for
happiness is a dream," he wrote in the _Gaceta_ of November
6. And in a strong article of the 13th of the same month, he
said: "Even those who confuse sovereignty with the person
of the Monarch must be convinced that the meeting of
representatives from the towns cannot be limited to the
narrow objective of nominating governors without the
establishment of a constitution by which they will be ruled.
The authority of the Monarch returned to the peoples
through the captivity of the King; the people can, therefore,
modify or reduce that authority to the form most agreeable
to them in the act of entrusting it to a new representative:
the king had no right whatever because, until now, no social
pact has been contracted with him ... The Laws of the
Indies were not made for a nation and already we are
forming one ...."

And two days later he wrote: "The Spanish towns, well

and good, kept themselves dependent on the prisoner King, awaiting his freedom from captivity and his return; they established the monarchy, and since the present prince is a descendent of the royal line which, by express pact with the Spanish nation should reign over them, he had the right to claim the observance of the social contract at the time that it is expedient for him to fulfill his part of the contract. America can in no way consider herself bound by that obligation; she had not been a party to the celebration of the social pact through which the Spanish monarchs derive the only titles to the legitimacy of their rule . . ."

In Moreno's written works the invocation of the "general will" and the "social pact" is frequent. Admirer of Rousseau, he wrote a preface to a reprint of *The Social Contract* from which he eliminated the last chapter entitled *La Religion Civil.* "As the author," he says, "had the misfortune to go astray in religious matters, I suppress the chapter and principal passages which touch on this subject."

In Moreno there persisted the deeply religious sentiment of his childhood, a sentiment which had stimulated, in both his parents and his teachers, the desire to see him ordained a priest. The ecclesiastical career was for him something more than a vague plan since, after he graduated in theology at the beginning of 1801, he received—the next year—the dimissory letters for the tonsure and lesser orders. Manuel Moreno, in his biography of his brother, frequently cited in the pages that follow, tells of his parents' disillusionment on learning that Mariano had enrolled as a student of law. His later marriage in Chuquisaca removed all hope.

A tender letter from Fray Cayetano to Moreno, recently published, is proof of the displeasure of the parents over the marriage of this son whom they had destined for the Church.

Moreno's father, dying in November, 1805, never had the chance to see his firstborn as leader of the *Junta de Gobierno*. On the other hand, fate spared him the sorrow of his son's death, far from his native land, far from his home, without the consolation of being surrounded by his dear ones before closing his eyes forever. Fate gave him for a tomb the infinite sea.

His premature and tragic death continues to rouse the profound sympathy of posterity for the great man of May. But the permanence of his memory rests not only on sentiment awakened by a life cut off through the cruelty of destiny. Man of thought and of action, idealist and pragmatist, the brilliant Secretary, if he did not figure among the rebels of the first hour, nevertheless identified himself with the revolution, and from the *Junta* was its soul and its guide. For that—in spite of isolated detractors without echo in public opinion—Moreno, 150 years after his death, continues to live in the conscience of Argentine generations, who recognize and revere him among the illustrious founders of the nation.

Mariano J. Drago

Buenos Aires, September, 1962.

The late Dr. Mariano J. Drago was a member of the National Academy of Law and Social Sciences of Buenos Aires, ambassador and permanent representative of the Argentine Republic to the United Nations, and Minister of Foreign Relations and Culture.

Preface
by Richard T. McCormack

The Undying Flame is the description that Ellen Garwood has given to Mariano Moreno, one of the revolutionary heroes of Argentina. The description could just as aptly be applied to the author herself, however, for Ellen Garwood has worked tirelessly all her life in behalf of the ideals in which she believes.

Mrs. Garwood is the daughter of the late William Clayton, a fascinating individual and a classic American success story. Born to poor parents in rural Mississippi, and almost entirely self-educated, he went on to found the Anderson-Clayton Company which became the world's leading trader in cotton.

A generous man and a genuine patriot, Mr. Clayton resolved to repay the country that had been so good to him. He volunteered his services to the Truman Administration and was given the position of Under Secretary of State for Economic Affairs. It was while serving in this position that he made his most notable contribution—the conceptual work behind the Marshall Plan.

Mrs. Garwood has carried on her father's tradition as a staunch advocate of free enterprise, open trade among nations and an interdependent world community of nations linked by commerce and mutual respect.

Mariano Moreno is a fitting symbol of Mrs. Garwood's approach. The young Moreno was a passionate believer in democracy, free markets, and free trade—in the system that today we call democratic capitalism.

Moreno and his achievements deserve to be honored not only in his native Argentina but throughout Latin America and the United States. The publication of Mrs. Garwood's book is thus a most welcome event.

The Undying Flame also appears at a propitious time. Given Argentina's recent return to democratic government, the story of Moreno has much of value to say as the country seeks solutions to the economic and political problems that confront it.

Readers in the United States will also find *The Undying Flame* a useful primer on Argentine history and a valuable reminder of the common economic and political traditions shared by both nations.

Mariano Moreno was a man who died more than 170 years ago, but his insights and principles are as relevant today as they were then. To him and to Ellen Garwood, who has so carefully nurtured that flame, we owe our gratitude.

Introduction

Mariano Moreno laid the groundwork for the coming of the military hero of Argentine independence from Spain, General José de San Martín. Without the advent of Moreno's organizing genius, the early days of the revolution of 1810, according to the historian José Ingenieros, would have been "shipwrecked in a sea of paper." It was Moreno who, more than anyone else in Buenos Aires, blazed the trail of freedom for which, upon going into exile in 1811, he predicted a long life. "I am going away," he said, "but the trail I leave behind me will be long!"

Moreno was a believer in freedom of trade and freedom of the press. He wrote a famous treatise on the former — his brief in defense of the ranchmen — and the first article ever to be published in his native land on the latter. While in his day he was best known outside the Viceroyalty because of the wide dissemination of his brief, *La Representación de los Hacendados*, which was published in London, a still greater work awaited him in his position as Secretary of State and of War in the revolutionary Junta of 1810. In this position he kept the torch of independence lighted long enough to rekindle the flame which had already flickered and wavered in Caracas. By the time Moreno's revolutionary career had begun, the colonial Junta in Caracas had started beating time by sending its most illustrious member, Simón Bolívar, on a mission for aid to London.

While the later military triumphs of Bolívar and San Martín in the northern and southern parts of the continent are well known, ending in the famous conference at Guayaquil 1821 with the generosity of the liberator San Martín toward Bolívar, still the figure of Moreno, revered by comparatively few writers — commemorated by a Plaza, a monument and a street in Buenos Aires — has, for years, remained an enigma. Only now the importance of Moreno's advocacy of free trade, as a source of income without which the colony could not have gained independence, begins to receive its just salute. With the spread of the "Common Market" principle among free nations in Europe as a force to roll back poverty and its attendant communism, the ahead-of-his-time Moreno emerges ever more clearly. And the principle remains true even when the planned destruction of Central America with its recently budding Common Market marches apace under the subversive tactics of Marxist guerrillas from Cuba and Nicaragua who are supplied by the Soviets.

Together with the importance of his devotion to freedom of trade, another factor has influenced me to write about Moreno. This phenomenon is that of the strong differences of opinion as to his character, evidenced most dramatically on the one hand by Pablo Groussac, best known for his biography, *Santiago de Liniers,* and on the other by Ricardo Levene, author of the detailed and scholarly *La Revolución de Mayo y Mariano Moreno.* According to Groussac it was evil sophistry in Moreno to order on July 28, 1810, the court-martial of the counter-revolutionary leaders headed by Liniers when these leaders were simply being true to the Spanish monarchy which the colonial revolution of 1810 mistrusted (in part because of its collusion with Napoleon), but for political reasons pretended to support. But as Levene emphasizes, the court-martial carried out on August 26 (at Cabeza del Tigre) "can be explained as the end of a trial imposed by the unfolding of events," thus implying that Moreno and the Junta, if they were to keep the revolution for independence alive, had no choice. And indeed such must be the conclusion of the objective historian when considering the threatened simultaneous blockade of Buenos Aires from those royalists in Montevideo who were helping the counterrevolution.

Today, Moreno's decision to keep freedom alive at whatever cost has a special relevance for those who must make the hard decisions of preserving a country's freedom against the attacks of a dictatorship that seeks world rule in a still more sinister way than those early nineteenth-century attempts of Napoleon.

My purpose has thus been prodded not only by the similarities of Moreno's problems to those of freedom's leaders today, but also by the desire to tell Moreno's story in such a way as to attract the attention of the general reader who is interested in the evolution of those rare figures of history responsible for the advancement of self-government. While the characters and incidents are all historical, there are, here and there, passages of imagined dialogue. But in every case this dialogue is connected with recorded events and often contains expressions used by Moreno, as documented in the works of Vicente López, Manual Moreno and Ricardo Levene. The conversation between Moreno and López (Chapter VIII, page 104) for instance, about Leiva's having miscounted the votes at the *Cabildo Abierto* of May 22, 1810, is straight from López who reports how Moreno had said of Leiva words to the effect that "if you count on that *comodin*, you'll see how he'll betray us. On one side or the other he'll wash his hands like Pilate." Levene recounts also, as do many other historians, how Moreno said as he left Buenos Aires in 1811, "I am going away, but the trail I leave behind me will be long." The author has invented only an elaboration of this saying in Moreno's probable explanation of it to his puzzled and distressed five-year-old son.

Among the several people to whom I am grateful for assistance are the following: the late Frances Hudspeth, of the University of Texas *Quarterly*, for her help with research materials; Dr. José Antonio Mendia, el Señor Garcia-Godoy, Mr. James C. Roberts, as well as Dr. Alma Lowe and Mr. Charles Smith (of St. Edward's University) for their suggestions and careful reading of the manuscript; Dr. Cupertino del Campo, for permission to use his portrait sketch of Moreno and to quote from his book, *Mensajes Liricos*; Dr. Alberto Prando, for introduction to invaluable sources of information in Buenos Aires; Sr. Arturo Fraser, for his help with Buenos Aires sources; Dr. Alberto Palcos, Dr. Bonifacio del Carril, Sra. Maria Elena Williams Balcarce de Moreno and Dr. Ivan Moreno for their interest and information about Moreno's family and associates; Sra. Estela de Martín for aid in research; Dr. Mariluz Urquijo for information about Chuquisaca; Dr. Julio Cesar Gonsalez, Director of the Historical Archives of the College of Philosophy and Letters of the University of Buenos Aires, for permission to use the archives and for making possible the photographs used in the book. I also wish to thank Sr. Ramon Pardo for permission to quote from his selected collection of documents from the Moreno family archives, issued in book form under the title "Mariano Moreno," with a preface by Luis Peralta Ramon, and sponsored by the *Instituto Bonaerense de Numismatica y Antiguedades*, to celebrate the 150th anniversary of the Revolution of May, 1810. And I am most grateful for the careful editing of Marc Lipsitz, and also for the interest and enthusiasm of Luis Alvarez of the Fundación Carlos Pellegrini.

—*Ellen Garwood*
Austin, Texas

I

Early Schooling
In Buenos Aires

"Mariano Moreno is a Jacobin!" — *pasquín,* or anonymous lampoon, pasted on the adobe wall running behind the Cathedral of Buenos Aires.

"Moreno is a man of low sphere, ugly words, and plotting soul" — unsigned notice, zigzagging across the back wall of the Cabildo — the Town Hall — which flanks the inland side of the *Plaza de La Victoria.*

"Moreno is a Demon of Hell!" — sign scrawled on the back fence of a shop formerly supplied by Spanish smugglers.[1]

Late November, 1810—summer already. A stifling, prematurely hot day—the kind of weather which, in Buenos Aires, precedes a pampero, kin to the Texas norther. On such a day one sees "demons" and experiences loss of faith.

Throughout the *Plaza de La Victoria* the signs against Moreno, who had led the city in its first steps towards independence these last few months, formed the subject of heated debate among knots of people gathered for shade and for a breath of air beneath the arches of the market *Recova,* the Cathedral, and the shops. Ranchers and gauchos, whose means of livelihood the lawyer had de-

fended, denounced the words as the plotting of jealous officials. Just who might be the particular authors?

"Could it be the Colonel?" one of the men ventured.
"We all know he's jealous."

"*Sí. Pero mas bien*, an agent from Cadiz, who hates free
trade. That's the pig who stuck up the *pasquín!*" A tall
hacendado thrust his arms above his head, menacing the
sky. "For a drop of rain. If Moreno could bring us rain. Air!"

"What about the victory for our troops in the North!"
His companion fanned himself with his hat. "Isn't that
enough, *hombre*? Suipacha! They captured the Spanish flag.
That's good!"

"Too good for some!" the first speaker cried. "Take the
Colonel, like I said. Saavedra—*el presidente*. Suipacha was
Moreno's work, prodding the army. But because of the victory, Saavedra takes the credit. He'd return us to the Viceroys and be Viceroy, himself. Plot, little brothers? There's
your plot!"

Among representatives of the old officialdom — the
Spaniards who, until recently, held all the positions of
importance—the tenor of discussion ran the opposite way.

"A man who's throwing out all the old values—Moreno.
Smart, but too smart. Couldn't someone arrange a medicine—a poison?"

"*Dios, amigo*! You have only to talk to the provincial
deputies. They're beginning to hate him. He wants them to
make a constitution and then go back home and call a vote.
To give the vote to plebeians. Speak to Dean Funes. The
deputies, they will knife him! A skinny victim — not much
blood. A fiery Jacobin. . . . Pssst! Out comes the fire. We can
light our bonfires with the sparks." Laughter. "The fires
where we'll burn his decrees!"

"Quiet, friend. There he goes, the demon. Look—on his
way to the fort. To his office. Now. We could do it now!"

The knifing in such a scene would have been easy. The "demon" was walking past without a bodyguard. He never used one.[2] On any day his enemies — few in number, but growing — could have assassinated him. Accompanied only by his younger brother, Moreno walked with an elastic step. One could tell Mariano from Manuel best by the difference in their glance. In the eyes of the former, a mercurial flash of recognition (called by his contemporaries *chispas*) ignited his response to greetings from his friends.

Moreno was a lawyer. In 1810 he was thirty-two years old. Of medium height, slender, olive complexioned, with a pensive student's brow, dark, curly hair, and an air of concentration that changed to sparkling — *chispeante* — alertness when he was speaking, he could pass neither for a demagogue nor for a terrorist. Since he was neither, he could be accused of neither openly, nor by anyone who would sign his name. His gift — and his undoing — was that he was logical, too soon. Logical and electrically persuasive — before the judge when he presented his case, before the people when he began to talk, his eyes reflecting the flashes of wit that played in lines of humor, about his lips, now curved, now firmed, emphatic with the hammer blows of truth. His position as Secretary, more important than that of the President of the Junta, made him a target. Once Moreno was "called to take a position in the revolution," he filled it, "mixing with the multitude, not in their midst, but at their head." [3]

The first child of Manuel Moreno Argumosa and Ana Maria Valle was born in Buenos Aires on September 3, 1778. Fortunately for this son's political career, his father— a native of Santander, Spain — decided to drop the second half of his name. The young Mariano became therefore simply Mariano Moreno, an easier sound to answer to when he started going to school. And, for a politician, a euphonious combination of syllables with a popular ring.

As a child he needed no prop to his popularity. Learning began for him not in the school house, but at home. It was his mother who taught him reading, and much else.

Ana Maria was *portēna*—born in Buenos Aires, the port of the Viceroyalty of the Río de La Plata. Daughter of the Treasurer of the *Cajas Reales*, she must have been an unusual woman for her day, when girls were taught embroidery and music in preference to books. Under her tutelage, Mariano began to recite, at an early age, long poems and complete chapters from the prose works which she either read to him herself, or taught him to read.[4]

The family marveled at the boy's memory, at the shading and emphasis with which he recited. Back of the child's facility can be glimpsed a rare and warm intelligence in the mother. Even the mother of Domingo Sarmiento, the second great democrat who enters Argentine history, apparently did not teach her son so much in the realm of letters. In the vivid record Sarmiento leaves of her, we learn that she could read and write, but that, from disuse, she had lost the practice of writing as she grew older.[5]

Following his mother's intruction, Mariano went to a primary school called the School of the King, whose teachers were paid by the government.[6] Here the boy supplemented what his mother had taught him by perfecting himself in writing and arithmetic, which, together with reading, made up the subjects of this modest school. The teaching did not last long for Mariano; at the age of eight he caught smallpox.

In those days, before the introduction of vaccine in Buenos Aires, this disease was the chief terror of the mothers of young children, many of whom died from it each year. Mariano, surrounded by the love and solicitude of his family, fought valiantly against the illness, and, under his mother's constant vigilance and care, he conquered it. But, although they were barely perceptible, he bore the marks all his days. And he bore the memory, for in 1810, he introduced the permanent distribution of vaccine.

During the next four years (a blank in the biographies) both Ana Maria and Don Manuel doubtless set aside part of their time for the instruction of this favorite son whom they had destined for the priesthood, one of the few positions of eminence open to a *criollo*, as a man born in the colonies was called. They also introduced him early to Brother Cayetano Rodríguez, who conducted classes in the Franciscan monastery.

The street leading to the monastery was called San Francisco, and passed just one block south of the Plaza Mayor, the great Plaza which overlooked the river. Today this street bears the name of Moreno. It was here, west of the Plaza, on San Francisco, that the Morenos lived. Mariano visited the monastery often to read under the direction of Fray Cayetano, and when he went with his father he doubtless crossed the Plaza first, where Don Manuel had his office.

The Plaza Mayor was the nerve of the city's life — a panorama of color and movement, of confusion and noise. Since 1776 it had gained a new dignity with the elevation of the "Provinces of the Río de La Plata" into a viceroyalty. This viceroyalty was a huge, unwieldy territory, covering land now occupied by Argentina, Uruguay, Paraguay and Bolivia. Buenos Aires had been named the capital because it was the principal port, situated at the mouth of the La Plata river, practically on the Atlantic. Up until 1776 the port had been used chiefly as a military base to supply commanders who would make encroachments on the holdngs of the Portuguese in Brazil.

Instead of a military governor, there was a Viceroy who

presided over the Plaza at the time of Moreno's boyhood. He lived in the huge fortress of massive, grayish stone on a bluff which hugged the river side of the Plaza: a fortress palace, complete with medieval moat and drawbridge. The buildings that were fortified back of this moat comprised, besides the palace—on whose lower floor were the rooms of the *Audiencia* or Court—an armory, a treasury where Don Manuel worked, a supply building and quarters for the Vice-regal guard. From the upper floor of the palace there projected, on the inland side, an iron grilled balcony, guarding a long window which looked out towards the arcaded building of the Cabildo, at the far oposite end of the Plaza.

This Cabildo, or Town Hall, was also imposing, with upper and lower galleries and a tower in the center, rising like a spire, high above the rest of the building. The tower held both a clock and a bell, the principal use of which in the old days was to call the people together in case of an Indian raid or some other emergency. Later the bell would be used for Open Cabildo meetings. The Plaza, thus, was nearly closed at its two narrow ends by these two buildings. The longer sides of the oblong were more open. Along one side could be seen, near the fort, a theater built by the Viceroy Vértiz, a small edifice called the Picket of San Martín which housed a kind of emergency guard, the palace of the Bishop, and the Cathedral with its porch of twelve white Corinthian columns. On the other side there extended, running coastward from the Church of San Ignacio, the elaborate houses of the Escaladas and the Riglos, the latter a two-storied mansion, the ground floor of which was rented for shops.

In the huge space between, the market was held. Gauchos and *hacendados*, or cattlemen, drove their ox-drawn wagons right up to the Plaza, anchored them in a corner, and hung up the meat and the hides they brought to sell on the large hooks protruding from these wagons. Broom boys, poultry venders, water sellers wound in and out among them, crying out their wares. And, setting up booths anywhere they wished, were the produce men and women, some of them simply squatting on the ground behind huge stacks of oranges, peaches, and melons, corn and lettuces and sweet potatoes and firewood. Once in a while an old soldier from the Spanish regiments, no longer fit for service, would push his perambulating table with its tray of trinkets — rosaries, mirrors, fans, statuettes — through the crowd. And sometimes, on a fiesta day, a Spanish señora, her face covered by the black lace veil hanging from her high comb, would tell the young negro slave who bore the pillow on which she kneeled in church, to buy for her one of the fans or statuettes that these men sold.

As a boy, Mariano was attracted by the old slaves with their gnarled sticks who sold candy, and by the masts of ships anchored in the harbor. According to the monopolistic trade laws, foreign ships could not sell their goods openly. A thriving activity of smuggling filled the gap. Spanish merchants, almost alone, benefited from this illegal trade. Mariano must have wondered about these ships and the lands they came from. He plied his father with questions as they walked together across the Plaza.

The boy could spot the Franciscan monastery from the Plaza because of its high, white tower. Still further back there shone another tower — that of the church of Santo Domingo. In fact the whole sprawling village of Buenos Aires, with its streets fanning out from the Plaza to the wide, open pampas on the west, became a panorama studded with church and monestary towers. In the Plaza, nuns, priests, and friars—the blue-robed Recoletans, white-clothed Dominicans and brown-hooded Franciscans—were as normal a sight as the soldiers of the Spanish garrison.

Mariano felt a special reverence for the friars because

of the Franciscan Brother Cayetano, whose favorite he was. Brother Cayetano, a young and ardent idealist, wished to bring about more freedom for Buenos Aires and felt restrained from the activity he longed for because of his friar's robe. Although Mariano, at the age of twelve, enrolled in the *Colegio de San Carlos*, a secondary school, he was not forgotten by Brother Cayetano. Mariano had been his brightest pupil in the monastery classes which the boy had visited after his illness. On Mariano the friar fixed his hopes.

The school of San Carlos was not so close to the Plaza as the monastery, and Mariano missed his trips across this center of the city's life, with its high officials, its soldiers and its market crowds. But in spring there were other things to attract him: the flowering peach and lemon and orange trees, and the nesting birds that multiplied in these orchard groves which stretched behind most of the flat-roofed, one-storied houses of the city.

As his mind was one of intense concentration, he did not let himself be distracted too much. Besides, he liked school, and Brother Cayetano, his tutor in Latin and poetry, had given him a mission. The school of San Carlos had its faults, but Mariano was so glad for the chance of higher instruction that, always conscious of the Franciscan's prodding, he could not complain.

San Carlos was a combination boarding and day school, where the day pupils were twice as numerous as the boarders. It was the one school offering instruction higher than the primary grades in Buenos Aires. In his life of Mariano, Manuel Moreno tells us that his brother was a day pupil because their father, with his growing family of children (which would reach the number of fourteen), could not afford the extra tuition for a boarder.[7] In this the young Mariano was lucky. He was able to escape, to a degree, the strict monastic regimen under which the school was run.

The *Colegio* was administered by a rector. The students, taught by the clergy, were prepared not to become citizens so much as to become friars or clergymen. Against this rigid slant there began to seethe a volcano of resentment. In 1796 the boarders revolted. During the night they ran out the unpopular teachers and pronounced themselves the owners of the school. How was this possible? In some way they had been able to gather together a quantity of old firearms. When the judges of the court came in a body to recapture the school for the rector, the young revolutionaries fired on the judges. Finally, it was necessary to send a company of the Viceregal guard to subdue them.[8]

Since Mariano was not a boarder he took no part in this revolt. But he heard exciting versions of it the next day. Younger boys were always coming to him for protection. Any student who had been unjustly accused of a part in the uprising undoubtedly came to him for help that day. His brother tells us that his standing up for such boys got him in real trouble, at times, with his teachers.

He continued in this rather tense atmosphere of resentment and discipline for six years. His studies comprised Latin, philosophy, and theology. But the school, according to Manuel, was worse, even, than the poor schools of Spain, particularly in the instruction of science and the new discoveries. Still it was the only *colegio* available and Mariano stuck it out. His performance at the graduating exercises, where he "was chosen to uphold the honor of the school in an act of Conclusions of Philosophy" and later "also in Theology" [9] was such that he attracted the notice of a powerful and rich visitor to the city.

Dr. Don Felipe Iriarte was a curate from the Archbishopric of Charcas who had stopped in Buenos Aires on his way to the Council of the Indies in Madrid. It was before this Council that he had been commissioned to push a case which all the curates of his diocese were defending in a body.[10] Of this case, Manuel Moreno says simply that the curates were objecting to the way the Royal High Court of Charcas oppressed them.[11] It is evident that this was one of the many cases in which the colonial officials wrangled with the churchmen over positions of preference in the numerous ceremonies of those pompous days of Spanish rule.

Whatever it was, ships out of Buenos Aires were delayed because of Spain's war with England in 1797; the curate had time to be introduced to the brilliant, eighteen-year-old boy by the beloved Franciscan friar, Brother Cayetano Rodríguez, who had taken Mariano under his wing; in the end the curate had time not only to be interested but to offer Mariano the opportunity of which he dreamed. Dr. Iriarte offered him the chance to go to the University of San Francisco Xavier in the town of Chuquisaca in Upper Peru where he could study, not only for the priesthood as the elder Morenos wished, but also for the law.[12] The curate would not only pay Mariano's tuition, he would arrange for him to live in the home of his friend, the Canon Don Mathías Terrazas.

The offer was providential. Without it the higher learning necessary to the development of Moreno's talents would not have been possible. It did not exist in Buenos Aires. In the capital of the Viceroyalty there was no university.

So far no enemies have appeared on the scene for Mariano. And the epithet "demon of hell," [13] which was applied to him in a letter written by Don Cornelio Saavedra—his political enemy of the year 1810—and was also used in the *pasquines*, is the last description to be thought of in connection with the young protege of Brother Cayetano and the curate, Dr. Don Felipe Iriarte.

What kind of town, what manner of government and of

people formed the background for this ardent student—suave, gentle and quick of answer, according to his brother; [14] brilliantly courageous defender of his country, according to the poem of the Franciscan who loved him; [15] "Jacobin" and "demon of hell," according to the Saavedristas whose vanity and ego he wounded?

At the time of Moreno's birth Buenos Aires was, in relation to more lucrative parts of Spain's overseas empire, a fairly unimportant fortress town, whose chief attribute was a good harbor on the La Plata river. In 1776 the town had been designated the capital of the newly created, supposedly transient Viceroyalty of the Río de La Plata. But the Spanish officials, who were sent over to hold temporary posts in the colonies, preferred assignments in the rich metal districts of Mexico and Peru to the less rapid possibilities for wealth on the grazing lands or pampas. Ironically, it was these which were to make such great fortunes, later, for an independent Argentina.

Thus, for many years, the Spanish rulers had held Buenos Aires to be of secondary importance. They had even made the town and the surrounding territory subject to the jurisdiction of Peru. Added to this was the humiliation of Peru's consistent attempt to keep the port of Buenos Aires closed to foreign commerce. Unfortunately, this policy had remained even after a change of government divisions in the colonies which upgraded Buenos Aires.

Up until 1778 the whole of Spanish South America had been divided into only four governmental departments. There were the Captaincy General of Chile, the Captaincy General of Venezuela, the Viceroyalty of Peru—to which the provinces of the Río de La Plata had belonged—and, dating from 1739, the Viceroyalty of New Granada.[16] In addition there existed in Central and North America the Captaincy General of Guatemala and the Viceroyalty of

Mexico. Then, with a more exact knowledge in Spain of the geography of the New World, it was realized that more division of government for the colonies was needed. And although the creation of the Viceroyalty of the Río de La Plata was part of the general system of reform of the Bourbon kings, the actual accomplishment was more a matter of accident.

King Carlos III wanted to give prestige to the commander of a powerful expedition, based in Buenos Aires, which should take La Colonia de Sacramento and Río Grande do Sul away from the Portuguese. Therefore, in 1776 he gave this commander, Don Pedro de Cevallos, the temporary title of Viceroy of the Río de La Plata.[17] When the expedition was completed (without the conquest of Río Grande) and a new official sent to Buenos Aires to take Cevallos' place, in 1778, the establishment of the Viceroyalty became permanent.

The new Viceroy, Juan José Vértiz, was a stroke of luck for Buenos Aires. He founded the school of San Carlos and he gave the city a public lighting system by replacing the old tallow candles with lanterns hanging from posts. Amazingly enough he founded a theater and dismissed the priest who warned the women against attending it. He founded, besides, a hospital for women, a house for beggars, an orphans' asylum, and, perhaps most valuable of all, he purchased and put to use a printing press "which had been idle for many years in the Jesuit Academy of Monserrat" in Córdoba.[18] Vértiz had a census taken which gave the city about 25,000 inhabitants and the adjacent country about 13,000.[19] These figures covered the period between 1778, when Vértiz took office, and 1784, when he was succeeded by the Marquis de Loreto.

Loreto was the first Viceroy whom Mariano Moreno remembered. Very different in his manner from the direct and democratic Vértiz, who came from Mexico, the Spaniard Loreto ruled with haughty hand, with that pomp and ceremony which was so often more overpowering in the far-flung villages of the colonial provinces than back in Spain itself. One of his processions was so awesome with the goldbraided soldiers preceding and following the Vice-regal carriage, that Mariano, at age six, dropped on his knees before the cortege as it passed down his street. In all innocence he had taken the Viceroy for the Bishop and was kneeling to be blessed.[20]

Certainly during and before the early days of Mariano's childhood, Buenos Aires had lived a constrained and para-doxical life. Like the other colonial cities of Spain, she was weighted down with officialdom, with church ceremony and emphasis on the outward cult of religion. Unlike the others, she was gifted with a combination of productive ranch-farm land and a temperate climate. The result was the creation of ranching and agricultural pursuits, both conducive to the development of a strong, independent personality. Unlike the others, too, her population was more white than Indian, for the Indians were much more numerous in the mining districts. These features, coupled with her advantageous position as a port at the mouth of La Plata, opening into the Atlantic, gave the new Viceroyalty an orientation towards a wider as well as a more self-assertive role in history than she would otherwise have had. But always there is that con-flict in the Argentine soul which reflects the struggle be-tween the country's natural advantages for democracy and world affairs and the heavy habit, the long colonial tradition of absolute subservience to form and power.

During the days in which Mariano grew up, the *porteño* —the inhabitant of the *port* of Buenos Aires—had begun to experience a sudden lift to the feeling of his importance as an individual. This realization was bolstered by a new intellectual ferment—a ferment that stemmed from the books of the French encyclopedists—Rousseau, Voltaire, Queznay— as well as from the Spanish liberals, Campomanes and Jovellanos and from the writings of two revolutionaries of North America, Paine and Jefferson. Here were books that exalted the individual and upheld, directly or indirectly, the idea that the only good government is that which reflects the voice of the governed.

As yet these new currents could be discussed only in secret in Buenos Aires. The reading of most of the books was forbidden by the Inquisition. Although Moreno could read what had been smuggled into the Franciscan library of Brother Cayetano, it was natural for him to seek escape from the stifling atmosphere which made open championship of such theories a crime.

He would not find less narrowness in Chuquisaca. But at least the university life there would offer him wider discussion with other seekers after truth. He might discover that the spirit and even the letter of the laws he would study were more liberal than their application. Moreno, always an advocate of the enlightened middle-of-the-road, may have already been thinking, at the age of nineteen, how a bloodless revolution could be effected through a more just interpretation of the laws. But how could he possibly proceed to bring this about? This, he knew, was the mystery he must solve.[21]

II

Atmosphere of Town, Country and Family in Buenos Aires

"The difference in resources did not create a difference of class, because no class was dependent on any other for its food or for owning its own home. . . . This was always a characteristic of Argentine life, from Buenos Aires to Salta and Mendoza. The usual family of the creole was always owner of an urban lot, of a quarter of a block, at least, planted with peach trees, which provided it with firewood, and where the birds multiplied. For this reason there prevailed in the Argentine colony the habits of a democratic life. . . . " — López, Vicente F., *Historia de La República Argentina*, Vol. 1, p. 505–506.

"The Argentine family before the Revolution of May was characterized by the strong union of its many members and by the centralization of authority in the father, similar to that of the Castilian family of great traditions and examples." — Levene, Ricardo, *Historia de Moreno*, p. 30.

"The almost perfect rectangle of 22 blocks from north to south and east to west in. . .Buenos Aires, with its streets almost always full of mud, its brick-paved walks outlined by posts, its low, wide houses, some at a very different level from others, many adorned with great, jutting iron

balconies, must have seemed to the young Manuel
Moreno Argumosa (recently escaped from his
shipwreck near Tierra del Fuego) something like
paradise...." — Galvan Moreno, C., *Mariano
Moreno*, p. 15.

The Buenos Aires that Mariano would soon be leaving
was built along streets—muddy roads for the most part—
which radiated inland and sideways from the *Plaza Mayor*
on the river. These streets were crossed by others in an immense checkerboard, the farthest boundaries of which
marked the edges of a gigantic, unfurled fan of settlements
opening onto the pampas. Many of the streets were named
according to the principal buildings for which they were
famous. One street was called *Las Torres*, because of the
towers of its many churches; another, which boasted the
Post Office, was named *Correo*, the street of the mail; still
another, *Colegio* Street, that of the school. The provincial
earmarks of the colonial village thus stand out in this telling
designation of streets according to their most important
service to the town.

It was near the river that the clusters of residences
showed thicker. Some of them, belonging to wealthy
Spaniards, bore the family coat of arms engraved in the
stucco above the heavy, carved front door. And all the
houses, even the poorest, were graced with an inner patio,
many of them boasting windows with iron grill work, and a
back yard which was usually a peach orchard, with here and
there a golden acacia tree or a red-blossomed ceibo.

As the fan widened outward to the wild, open country,
the groups of houses were broken up by plots of ground set
aside for plazas. Among these there stands out the *Plaza de
Lorea*, where the Indians of the Pampas tribes, in their col-

orful striped blankets and turbans, held a market. Other interesting plazas were the *Plaza Nueva* for carts from the estancias, the *Plaza San Nicolas*, a monastery plaza connected with the church of the same name, and the *Plaza Monserrat*. It was in *Monserrat* that a permanent amphitheater was built in 1790, so as to afford a place other than the *Plaza Mayor* for the celebration of bull fights.[1] Bullfights were rare because the Bishops frowned on them. In fact, if the Cabildo had not been denied the use of public funds to give a celebration for the arrival of a new Viceroy, a permanent bullring might never have been erected.[2] It was the idea of the Cabildo that the proceeds from the permanent bullring would help pay for the sumptuous festivities by which they wished to impress the Viceroys — and thus, Monserrat.

One begins to wonder how it was possible to find much diversion in this colonial village, where customs and entertainment, to say nothing of learning, were so strictly regulated by the authorities. Only the Puritan strictness of the early New England settlements seems more stifling. True, there was more gaudy and brilliant color in Buenos Aires, where the red and yellow of the Spanish flag repeated itself in costumes at Carnival time, and where even religious processions of rigid formula were relieved by the blue and white and brown robes of the monks. Occasionally, too, there were masked dances, conducted by an impresario who rented for this purpose the *Ranchería*, an enclosure which used to house the slaves that were bought and sold by the Jesuits, before their expulsion in 1767.[3] And so there were both color and music, strictly under the guidance of the city officials.

Yet this pleasure to the eye and ear could not make up for the pincer-like grip on the expansion of the mind. Even in New England the Puritan rigidity was mitigated by freer

access to books and greater participation of the citizens in
the town council.

In Buenos Aires, Cabildo membership was predomi-
nantly Spanish. Up until 1809, few men born in the colonies
could be members of the Cabildo unless they were descendants of the conquistadores or owners of considerable property. In many towns, members of the Cabildo were appointed by the king. Added to this, the restriction of
legitimate trade to selling and buying from Spain piled insult upon injury.

Mariano heard much about these problems in the con-
versations of the older people with whom he spent so much
time in these days. One subject uppermost in everyone's
mind was the trade monopoly which was being debated in
the Consulate—a name applied, then, to a body somewhat
similar to the modern American Chamber of Commerce. It
was actually a kind of Merchants' Guild, more amenable to
the Spaniards than to the native sons. Yet ever since its
establishment in 1794 with young Manuel Belgrano as its
director,[4] there had been attempts by farmers and hacendados to convince the authorities to open the port to free
trade for their products. These arguments were encouraged and entered into by Belgrano—only nine years older
than Mariano. For on his return to Buenos Aires from Spain,
where he had graduated in law, Belgrano had brought with
him Condorcet's Spanish translation of Adam Smith's
famous *Wealth of Nations* with its thesis of free trade. Here
was a seed that would later aid in producing one of Mariano
Moreno's masterpieces, *La Representación de los Hacendados*—the Representation of the Ranchmen.

Meanwhile, all the debates about how to soften the evils
of the Spanish monopoly, with the out and out smuggling
that attended it (much as bootlegging became a twin of Pro-
hibition in the United States so much later), met with little

success. Yet in the years 1798 and 1799, when Napoleon became First Consul of France and increased his demands on his ally, Spain, in the war against England, Spain's ships of supply to the colonies were being almost entirely cut off by the British navy.[5] The Spanish monopoly of trade thus became a complete denial.

In view of this situation, what could have been the reason for the Consulate's and Cabildo's opposition to legalized commerce with neutral ships, authorized from time to time by the Spanish Court? The monopolist merchants of Buenos Aires, almost all Spaniards, were making so much money out of "contraband" goods (the influx of which they could control, making purchases under cover and against the law from the British, Dutch and other foreigners) that they would not hear to having trade, even with other colonies, declared legal and open. Shameful, because, even with a customs' duty, which would have cut deeply into their profits, the ample supply to the markets of the legal goods would have created a drop in price. It meant nothing to the Spaniards that the colonial treasury, always in need of funds, would gain from the customs' revenue, and that the people as a whole would benefit. If a man had come to Buenos Aires to make a killing out of the accepted practice of contraband trade, these considerations weighed little.

Because of this attitude, enlightened young men, who took the good of the colony to heart, carried on, from year to year, a losing battle for free trade. The arguments of such lawyers as Manuel Belgrano and Juan José Castelli, and the engineer Pedro Cerviño, availed nothing. There was nothing they could do to help even the hacendados, the owners of ranches and cattle, who were prohibited from selling hides and tallow to neutrals when outlets for these products to Spain were closed by the intermittent wars with

England. Yet it was these hacendados who were the hardest hit, since not only their supplies were raised in price, but their ability to pay for them was strongly curtailed with the door closed to legal exports. All the while smuggling of imports went on and prices soared. In 1799, British linen went up ten reales, and salt, paper, cooking oil, sugar, glass and steel, rigging and tar were listed as nearly doubled in price.[6] It is hard to see how the hacendados gained a livelihood in this period, with 600,000 cattle slaughtered a year and the local market consuming the meat and other products of only 150,000.[7] In spite of the hacendados' pleas to the court in 1794 and later, the twins of monopoly and smuggling flourished.

Mariano's father did not take much part in the discussions about free trade. Nevertheless, because of his position as clerk in the Royal Treasury, a place similar to the one his father-in-law had held before him, he did realize how much revenue the treasury was missing with the increase in contraband goods. Here was a dilemma. The tenure of his position depended on his getting along with the colonial authorities. What should he do? One receives the impression that the elder Moreno's exercise of moral, as well as physical, courage had reached its height before he settled in Buenos Aires.

Mariano's father, it is true, belonged to a rather less frequent type of Spanish immigrant than the usual kind who came to the colonies. The usual immigrant fell into one of three classes. First there were the government employees who, with the exception of tax officials whose appointments were for life, were birds of passage, sent over for a short time to make a killing and scatter it later back in Spain. The second class was larger and was composed of merchants attracted by the ease with which they could make a respectable living. They usually remained in the colony and married some creole girl with a dowry. The third and largest class were adventurers, many of whom had come to America to escape the vigilance of the law in Spain. Although these last were looked down on at first, the superiority connected with the mere fact of being a Spaniard often elevated them to equal positions with the other two. Between the first two and the third there were a few immigrants who had obtained permission from the government for specified reasons, and whose only pay was a reduction in the price of passage.[8] Mariano's father belonged to this class.

He had first decided to come to America in order to gain a better livelihood than he could expect from following in the footsteps of his parents who were laborers in Santander, but who, nevertheless, were "full of the presumption of an aristocratic origin, as were all the natives of that part of Spain." [9] Before coming to Buenos Aires the elder Moreno had gone to Havana as private secretary to an old general. When the general died he left his savings to his secretary. It was after providing for his parents from this small sum that Don Manuel, exhibiting that mixture of thoughtfulness and daring which his son, Mariano, was to display later in the field of government, took his fate in his hands and set out for Buenos Aires.

Here he entered the service of a merchant who procured for him the place of ship's clerk in a vessel setting sail for Lima. Unfortunately, this ship was wrecked on Cape Horn, near Tierra del Fuego. Don Manuel barely escaped with his life. Finally, by the aid of some kindly Indians with whom he made friends, he was able to put one of the lifeboats into good enough condition to return him to Buenos Aires.

The elder Moreno did not like to speak much of this shipwreck. Yet he never forgot his gratitude to the poor Indians of Tierra del Fuego. Soon after this experience, on his return to Buenos Aires, he married, took the opening offered to him as clerk of the Royal Treasury, and probably determined never to leave dry land again. About the Indians who had helped him he frequently told stories to his family, thus planting early in Mariano a desire to better the severe conditions under which the Spaniards held the Indians subject—not so much in Tierra del Fuego as in other parts of the Viceroyalty.

In the lines written by Mariano's brother, Manuel, their father is seen as an honorable man of unswerving honesty, as well as of generous heart. He was also a man of above average skill in figures and diplomacy, since he was chosen to be one of the accountants or ministers of *hacienda* in a boundary commission sent out about 1784 to fix the demarcation line between Spain's and Portugal's territory — between the Viceroyalty of the Río de La Plata and the Portuguese settlements in Brazil. With these qualities went an unusual modesty and economy of speech.

The elder Moreno did not push himself forward to gain any extra prize for his service with the boundary commission, as some of the other members, who exercised pull at the Court, had done. And although the additional money he had earned allowed him to buy a decent house in town, with slaves, when he returned to Buenos Aires,[10] he had to go back to his old position of treasury clerk with no raise in his meager salary of 600 pesos a year. He does not seem to have complained but, instead, to have become overstrict in matters of amusement so as to hold down expenses and live within his income. This was understandable for a man whose family was growing every year and was eventually to reach the number of fourteen children.[11]

Still it is a happy family circle that appears in Manuel Moreno's *Life and Memoirs of Dr. Don Mariano Moreno*.

While the elder Moreno forbade dancing and cards, he was devoted to his wife and children. Every day after his work in the treasury he came home to lunch at two o'clock. In the evenings he entertained a group of friends whose talk centered mostly around history and travel and the latest news of public affairs.[12] The elder children took part in these gatherings, which lasted as late as eleven o'clock in summer and ten o'clock in winter, at which time a light supper was served. A half-hour later the parents and older children retired.[13]

As Don Manuel did not like to cater to those above him, he preferred to invite to his house, not the higher officials of the colony, but men who were his equals in station and income. We can imagine him entertaining schoolmasters and priests; scholarly men such as Dr. Manuel Labarden, examiner in the courses of philosophy at San Carlos,[14] and Dr. Pantaleon de Rivarola, chaplain of one of the Viceroy's regiments. He probably also invited the engineer Pedro Cerviño, who doubtless complained at the way science was taught, or rather was *not* taught, except in vague theory, at San Carlos. It was Cerviño who was to become, in 1799, director of the *School of Navigation*, the founding of which had been influenced by Belgrano. Cerviño may also have discussed the monopolistic trade laws. And it is possible that a few ranchers came to the house and discussed them, too.

However, if Mariano, in these days, heard very much about the injustices of colonial rule, it is more likely that he heard such talk in his close association with Brother Cayetano Rodríguez. The year after Mariano graduated from San Carlos he spent most of his time with this ardent Franciscan, who had picked him out, as a child, to be a leader. Brother Cayetano offered him free access to the monastery library. Here was a wealth of knowledge, for the

Franciscan order, which played a great role in the revolutionary movement throughout Spanish America, was one of the chief importers of forbidden books. The monks could manage this importation with a fair degree of safety by arranging for their agents abroad to send the books in boxes marked "sacred ornaments." With access to such learning Mariano could read Paine and Jefferson, both of whom he quotes many years later in his articles in the *Gaceta* of 1810, which he founded. In certain issues of the *Gaceta* we see him also publishing not only a reprint of a Spanish translation of Rousseau's *Social Contract*, but parts of Jefferson's *Notes on Virginia* as well.

As the great gap between the worth of the individual, which shines in these pages, and the status of the colonial or creole in Buenos Aires flashed into the young boy's receptive mind, the injustice of the trade monopoly stood out most glaringly. Although Mariano was, like his father, neither obsequious nor pushy, this does not mean that he was not practical, as his father had been in the strict balancing of his accounts. And it is this practical idealism of Mariano's which showed him early on that all the ills of the colony—the backwardness in education, in self-government and in care for the unfortunate Indians and half-breeds, and even laxness in the development of new industries and arts —were, in large part, directly traceable to a lack of public funds due to the stagnation of trade and the barefaced practice of smuggling.

It may be asked why the custom of slavery did not bother him more. (The slave trade, in fact, was the only "foreign trade" which the monopolists did not fight.) The answer to Moreno's stronger emphasis on other injustices is found in the fact that slavery was much less a hard and fast condition in Buenos Aires than it was in the young United States. In the first place there was no large crop in the Río de La Plata region so dependent upon slave labor as was cotton in the south of North America or sugar in north-eastern Brazil. In the second place, a slave, in Buenos Aires, could engage in a small, independent business outside his work for his master and in this way often earn enough money to buy his freedom.[15] In fact, the lot of the slaves was much happier than that of some of the descendants of the Incas, who were forced to work the silver mines in long shifts or mitas, for miserable pay. These Indians, or mitayos — so called because of the mitas they served — became known to Mariano later when he went to school in Chuquisaca (the present Sucre, Bolivia), a town situated near that part of the Andes where the mines were richest.

In his pre-university days it was not the life of the slave but that of the middle-class, intelligent creole (man of Spanish parents, born in the colonies) which looked most hopeless. Yet to the casual observer or to the happy-go-lucky materialist, the colonist had nothing too serious of which to complain. If he never wished to advance, if he had no thirst for truth, no curiosity about the outer world, it could be said that he lived a fairly comfortable life. Mariano felt this, too, and pondered, at times, whether the challenge was great enough to make him risk his neck to set things right. He almost said as much to his brother years later, the night Manuel brought him the news of his election as Secretary of Government (comparable to Secretary of State) in the new revolutionary Junta. "The rest which I've enjoyed until now in the midst of my family and my books will be interrupted," he said; and then added that, even so, if his country needed him, his personal considerations of comfort would weigh nothing.[16]

What was this restful, almost bucolic life that went on in the port city which lay on the edge of the pampas? This village life of official pomp and religious processions, occa-

sional bullfights and long siestas all faintly spiced by the circulation of gossipy *pasquínes* and the usual frontier hints of
danger from Indian raids? What was this life where even
the Indians, tamer than the North American tribes, were
often less to be feared than outbreaks of violence from
wandering bands of gauchos turned into outlaws and made
nomads because of the precarious position of the ranches?

Beneath the fairly placid life of Buenos Aires an under-
current of resentment continued to rise more and more
forcefully against the preference given to Spaniards over
creoles. All important positions—those of judges, tax collec-
tors, sheriffs, alcaldes, councilmen — were filled by
Spaniards. The Spaniards, partly because of this, were easily discernible from the men born in the country. They were
characterized by the heavier tread of their walk, their more
haughty demeanor, their more exaggerated and elegant
manners. On the other hand, the creoles exhibited an
elasticity of temperament and a greater vivacity. Certainly
they led a more active, outdoor life, and many of the young
men of good families, impatient at finding no opening in
public affairs, joined bands of gauchos and took to a
wandering, adventurous existence on the pampas.

Among these people there were slaves, as we have
seen, but they were all confined to domestic service. The
wealthy families owned ten or twelve, from waitresses to
washerwomen to ironers, from the handyman builder to the
coachman and tender of horses. And poor families possessed slaves, and even the negroes, themselves, owned
them. But they left them much of their time free, on condition they pay the master a fixed monthly sum. The slave, in
this way, often carried on business, selling cakes or fruit or
firewood, and after a while many of them were able to buy
their freedom. The historian Vicente Fidel López tells us
that they were very attached to the creole youth, whom

they followed and loved not only as models, but also as opponents of the influence and haughtiness of the Spaniards. In this the mulattos and the *chinos* (so called because of their yellow skin), who were offspring of the Guaraní Indians and the Spaniards, joined them.

This mixed population of white creoles, negroes, mulattos and chinos formed a fairly uniform moral mass since most of them were owners of their own homes. By 1800 they were developing "a true nationality with a spirit of its own, which called itself *hijos del pais*, or creoles, and which, with this name, divorced itself from the Europeans, ever since the creation of the Viceroyalty, with gradually increasing and accentuated spirit." [16]

It is no wonder, then, that the sensitive student, Mariano Moreno, in the year 1799, when he left for Chuquisaca, felt himself called upon not so much to correct slavery as to study law and government. He was thinking, even then, that he must find a way whereby this budding individuality and nationality, as described by the historian Vicente López, might realize itself.

III

Incident on the Road to Chuquisaca

Brother Cayetano "fixed his glance on Moreno first. . . because he appeared most ardent. In all great social transformations impulsive natures exercise a powerful, definitive role. He saw the boy's radiant look, his daring mien." To the Franciscan friar, Moreno "possessed the sacred fire, and he was not mistaken." Cayetano "did not create it, he awakened it. . . ." — O'Connor, Arturo Reynal, *Los Poetas Argentinos*, p. 306

At twenty-one, Mariano Moreno, brought up under a strict, affectionate discipline, began his first long trip away from home. The prospect that stretched before him of almost 2,800 kilometers—about 2,000 miles—on horseback, much of it through wild, unpopulated land, must have seemed hazardous as well as fateful.

According to his brother, Manuel, who heard the story later, Mariano on his first night of travel was tempted to turn back.[1] Even his desire to go to a university, kindled by Brother Cayetano, became, for the moment, secondary. In order to continue his journey he had to call up all his reserves of will and purpose.

It was a spring day of November, 1799. With two or three other travelling companions he had ridden horseback all day. That evening the party stopped to spend the night at one of the miserable huts on the postal route they were following. Mariano lay down on a cot and tried to sleep, but his companions were not looking for anything so peaceful. They called for drinks, gathered around a table, and drew out a pack of cards. Then they started gambling. With the gambling there began to break out quarrels, followed by fist fights, oaths, and obscenities shouted louder and louder.

Mariano tossed on his cot. Had he fallen among thieves? He fingered the jewels which his mother had thrust into his hands only that morning. He had protested against taking them but she'd insisted. He felt a little guilty, knowing that one of his aims in going off to study—that of learning law— was unknown to her and quite different from preparation for the career in the church which she was expecting for him. She had been determined that he take her jewels in case of an emergency. The money his father had given him was just barely enough for Mariano's travel fare and his food. (Later his father would procure for him, from the Viceroy del Pino, an exemption from the fee usually paid for a degree in theology.) As for his tuition at the university and his lodging, Dr. Iriarte had promised to take care of that. *Should* he have let his mother give him her jewels?

The voices of the gamblers became strident, threatening. He began to wish he had never left home. Would he ever see it again? Was he foolish to undertake so much—going off to study both for the church and for the law? What had started him in this direction, anyway?

He turned his body toward the wall, trying to shut out the light, the gambling table, the flashing knives, the noise. Had he left behind everything good? Was there strength in

honor, in truth? Where had he first known the uncom-
promising, the non-conformist truth?.... Brother Cayetano's classes... years ago.

The Franciscan friar used to walk up and down before
his young pupils and exclaim to them that the colony was
passing through sterile years.

"But," he would add, "I hear rumblings of liberty. My
sons, we must work. We must form men!" [2]

Mariano felt the friar's glance fixed on him. In many
ways they were kindred spirits. Unconsciously, he realized
now, he had modeled himself on Brother Cayetano. He
remembered how often the friar had combined an almost
maternal gentleness with a love of poetry and heroism. One
day he had found out that the Franciscan was writing
poetry of his own.

Brother Cayetano was only eighteen years older than
Mariano. He had not been born in Buenos Aires, but in the
village of San Pedro, on the banks of the Paraná river — a
village with few other settlers. As a youth he had been free
to wander over the countryside in the wilderness of wooded
ravine and pampa, with its high, waving, golden pampa
grass. Here he had conceived a love of nature which was
another trait he shared with Mariano, one of whose favorite
books was Bernadin de St. Pierre's *Studies of Nature*.

There was a Franciscan monastery in San Pedro. It was
here that the young Cayetano went to school and had been
inspired by the friars to become a friar himself. At the age
of sixteen he entered the monastery of San Francisco in
Buenos Aires, taking his vows one year later for the priesthood, in 1778, the year of Mariano's birth.

The memory of his boyhood freedom, in contrast to the
oppression exercised by such Viceroys as Loreto toward the
liberal Canon Maciel, caused feelings of revolt in Cayetano.
Maciel had advocated an innovative system of teaching at

San Carlos. He had argued that "in physics they should leave off Aristotle and follow Descartes and Newton and the obervation of experience, in which the modern academies work so usefully."[3] His advice was overruled. Later, when he dared to defend an archdeacon who had married a couple against orders of the Viceroy procured by the girl's father, and when the man who coveted the arch-deacon's place was a friend of this same Viceroy's, Maciel was sent into exile.

It was such injustices that aroused in brother Cayetano not only revolutionary sentiments, but seeds of doubt as to the expediency of his own calling in bringing about the needed reforms. If the most intelligent and liberal priests could be thrown out, perhaps it was better not to be a priest. As to his own role, there was no question. He had chosen this course, and he would not turn aside. But for the man of the future, for the leader he might fashion, that was a different story.

It was then, Mariano guessed, that the friar had begun to look among his pupils for a disciple of freedom.

"We must form men," he kept repeating. "Here before us is the patria, and a new century! We must dilate our minds and widen our hearts and invigorate ourselves with public life!" [4]

The words were resounding in the young traveler's ears. They drowned out the bets of the gamblers. Mariano's tossing subsided. Now the words became a whisper, but they were so clear that it was almost as if the brown-hooded figure were leaning over him. "Don't turn back. Keep on your way!"

Mariano sank into a half sleep. He was back at San Carlos. He remembered how he used to read so late after he came home from school that his parents often took his books away from him. At San Carlos he had made many friends,

mostly among the older boys. The younger ones, too, came
to him for protection. He remembered how his defense of
these boys would sometimes compromise him with his
teachers, but how he had not minded because he always
knew that Brother Cayetano approved. ("Any oppressed
child, even a stranger, would always find him at his side to
defend him," [5] his brother Manuel would say.) Again the
whispered words: "Keep on your way. It's your only chance
to study law . . . the first step in the struggle to form free
men."

He stirred on the narrow cot. The oaths of the gamblers
receded. . . . What — besides the voice of the Friar, which
was almost like his own—were his other assets? He began to
remember. In his luggage he carried, well-guarded, two
important notes from his new-found friend and patron, the
curate Dr. Don Felipe Iriarte. One of them requested the
protection of the Archbishop of Charcas for him in Chuquisaca. The other was a letter to the Canon Terrazas, who
would probably give him lodgings. In it, Dr. Iriarte had written: "I present to you a youth who will be a treasure and an
ornament to his profession, and who will repay with interest any favor shown him by the honor he will someday
bring upon his benefactors." [6]

Too much was expected of him to turn back. Between
his fitful dreams he waited out the night. The next morning
he was on his way again.

IV

Legal Training, Career and Romance in Chuquisaca

" 'Keep the land for the Emperor, my Señor, and let the Devil govern it!' This was the last instruction of the Supreme Council regulating the powers of Dr. Gasca when he went to America to calm the violent convulsions which threatened... Spain with its loss." — Moreno, Mariano, *La Representación de los Hacendados*, in *Escritos Politicos y Económicos de Mariano Moreno*, edited by Norberto Piñero, p. 124.

"...certain it is that the atmosphere and stuffy, barren situation of the mines, their intolerable odors and exhalations.... the smoke of the candles used for digging, can do no less than occasion... painful and even mortal illnesses.... Of the four parts of Indians who leave for the mita, there rarely return to their homes three entire parts.... All these mitas, where they are not expressly revoked by earlier cedulas, are totally annulled by the illegal conditions under which they are practised... only the miners of Potosí continue them, wishing to sustain with blood and fire a mita the most irregular and repugnant to the indisputable rights of the Indians." — Moreno, Mariano, *Disertación Juridica Sobre el Servicio personal de los Indios en General y Sobre el Particular de Yanaconas y Mitayos*, in *La Revolución de Mayo y Mariano Moreno*, by Ricardo Levene, Vol. 3, pp. 22, 24.

When the party with which he traveled toward Chuqui-saca reached the city of Tucumán, Mariano fell ill. The other travelers could not wait for him. He was left in care of the keepers of the post house.

Tucumán was about halfway between Buenos Aires and his destination. It lay in a semi-tropical valley at the foot of the Andes, in the northwest part of what is now Argentina. Fortunately, the post house was a little better than those of the smaller stopping places. It was in Tucumán that the wealthier travelers, who could afford to buy a coach for the trip, usually sold the conveyance to someone returning to Buenos Aires. This was done because much of the trip beyond Tucumán traversed the Andes and could only be made on the back of a mule.

As we have seen, Mariano had traveled from the beginning on horseback, the mode of travel most current at the time. Upon leaving Buenos Aires he had also paid a mounted postilion to lead the pack horse which carried his trunk. And starting out with him from the Plaza de Lorea, the place of departure on the outskirts of Buenos Aires, had been the two or three other men who had spent the night at the first post gambling and drinking.

The posts where the travelers stopped to change horses and spend the night were situated at places about ten or twelve leagues distant along the way. They were miserable ranch huts, for the most part, whose maintenance fell under the jurisdiction of the Buenos Aires *Administration of the Mails*.[1] In its efforts to improve things the Administration had limited itself to the issuance of circulars, ruling that the posts should keep a decent room destined for travelers only, with two cots on which to rest, and some provisions of food. But there was never any inspection to see if these orders were carried out. The result was that the *Masters of the Post* managed to do as little for the traveler as possible. If they could offer a meal consisting of roast meat and maté, and give the traveler or mail carrier a change of horses, they could get by. It was too bad if a man fell ill and had to wait over, for the post huts, with their loosely thatched roofs, were protected against neither rain nor insects.

Mariano had been growing more and more tired as the trip progressed. He was not used to the long rides of ten or twelve leagues a day. Nor was he used to the continual alternations of cold and heat, the drenchings in the streams he had to ford by swimming his horse, and the dry baking out later under an intense sun. He had crossed forests, desert, hills, and now, before him, a paradise of orange trees—a town heavy with the scent of flowers he could not enjoy. At Tucumán he became crippled with rheumatic fever.

Manuel Moreno, who later studied medicine at the University of Maryland in Baltimore, relates that there were no doctors in Tucumán, outside of a few quacks whose knowledge of cures was limited to bleeding. Mariano did not consult these *curanderos* but rather placed himself entirely in the hands of the keepers of the post. These people happened to be honest, simple folk and gave him what care they could in the fifteen days he remained with them. Later he would recall their kindness in lending him one of their mattresses, which they placed on the floor of the travelers' room. One of the family had to feed him since he was too weak, at first, to do this for himself. Always he remembered with gratitude their affectionate care. It was while he was sick here in Tucumán that his natural sympathies for the helpless and the sick among poor people everywhere were sharpened. The poor, consumptive Indians of the silver mines whom he would meet later would find a strong advocate and defender in him, partly due to his recollections of his own seemingly desperate illness at the post house.

One day he was overcome by thirst. At the time there was no one to wait on him. By slow degrees he worked over to the side of his mattress to reach a water jug that had been placed on the floor of the hut not far away. He was able to tip the jug over and drink, but his arms were too weak to right the jug again, so that the remaining water poured out, drenching him completely. Like as not his illness had been due, in part, to a nervous tension, for the shock of the cold water seems to have freed him eventually from his pain. The next day, wonder of wonders, he was able to take up his journey again.[2] He continued on his way by short stages, paying his postilion a little extra for the slowness of his going. After two and a half months he reached Chuquisaca. Such was the price a young creole of the year 1799 was willing to pay in order to receive a university education.

What were Mariano's impressions upon reaching Chuquisaca and being welcomed into the home of the wealthy canon, Don Mathias Terrazas? First of all, he was struck by the dramatic difference in the physical aspect of the town and that of Buenos Aires. Instead of being flat and spread out like his birthplace, this town, smaller than Buenos Aires, was hemmed in by wooded mountain peaks. It was situated in a sheltered hollow of the Andes, on a narrow plateau, like a natural stairway of trade between the provinces higher up in what is now Bolivia, and the lower provinces of the present Argentina. At its southeastern corner this plateau was accented by two conical peaks of porphyry or jasper, purple-red in color, rising one against the other like "mysterious sphinxes." [3] All around the town there grew beautiful forests, watered by two great riverways. For Chuquisaca, which in Indian means "Golden Bridge," was the central point between the Pilcomayo and the Guapay rivers.

The winding streets of the town were punctuated by

church towers, while the plazas, smaller and more intimate than those of Buenos Aires, were graced by splashing fountains. And here and there a broad street, such as the Prado which was lined with Tamarisk trees, began and ended in one of these beautiful plazas. In truth, the city of the Golden Bridge had the appearance of a resort town. And in many ways it was, for it was here that rich mine owners of the surrounding districts liked to spend their leisure time. As for the Canon's house which was to be his home, its chief attraction for Mariano was a remarkable library. Since Don Mathias extended to his young guest the same privilege he, himself, enjoyed of being free from censure by the Inquisition, Mariano was able to read whatever he wished. Among these books, prohibited for the general reader, were Bossuet's *Universal History*, Fleury's *Ecclessiastical History*, Fenelon's *Telemachus*, Raynal's *History of the Indies*, as well as volumes by Jovellanos, Bacon, Locke, and Montesquieu. There were, besides, countless manuscript works of the history of the Spanish conquest, including the famous *Comentaries of the Incas* by Garcilasso de La Vega, who claimed descent from the Indian nobles.[4]

Outside of his classes and the feast of reading afforded him by the Canon's library, Mariano's chief interest was in a club of students who held revolutionary ideas. Upon joining the club he became a devoted friend of the priest Francisco Medina, who was one of its leaders. At the same time he cherished his relationship with the Canon Terrazas who seems to have loved him as much as if he were his son. This was lucky, for Don Mathias was Assistant to the Archbishop, Don Alberto, and was able to distribute so much patronage that he came to be one of the most influential men in the province.[5] Because of this his house was continually visited by friends and seekers of favor, and he entertained lavishly. In spite of the fact that Mariano was not used to this luxurious life, or maybe because he was not, he won the Canon's heart.

He had been in Chuquisaca for over a year when he fell ill with a kind of rheumatic paralysis again. The Canon became so solicitous about Mariano's health that he ordered a servant to read to him every day. One night, when the Canon was giving a banquet for a magistrate from Spain, one of the houseboys secretly brought Mariano, against the doctor's orders, a plateful of sweets from the table. When Don Mathias found this out he was so worried about the effect on Mariano's health, and so angered, that he ordered fifteen lashes for the unfortunate servant.[6] Just as before Mariano had been made well by an accident, again he suddenly recovered after this breaking of his diet. And it is not unlikely that the thought of how he must right matters for the unlucky servant hastened his return to health.

There are indications in Manuel's biography of his brother that Mariano felt, in the midst of his gratitude to his patron, a genuine and mature sorrow, for one of his age, that the Canon should put so much stress on the exercise of his authority and power. There is little doubt that the sensitive boy tried to soften, at times, any undue harshness or trivial imposition on those below him to which Don Mathias might resort. Manuel Moreno must have had it from Mariano, for instance, that "the many conveniences of the Canon's house served him for nothing but ostentation, since all of his time was employed outside of it in business." [7] How different he was from Fray Cayetano!

Still Mariano took advantage of the fact that the Canon's house was the center of negotiations for many of the towns of the district because of its owner's connections. This circumstance helped him "acquire a singular skill in the management of affairs, and an exact knowledge of the human heart." "His observations," his brother tells us, "were so exact and penetrating that he was rarely deceived in judging men. . .a trait that was worth much to him in public office later." [8]

While Mariano was mixing with his patron's important friends and learning to evaluate them he was, at the same time, attending meetings of students who criticized these high officials with extreme bitterness. He listened with sympathy to his fellow students' complaints, and indulged in rather daring criticism himself in the skillful *Disertación Juridica Sobre el Servicio Personal de Los Indios en General y Sobre El Particular de Yanaconas y Mitayos*. It was at the Royal Academy of the Practice of Jurisprudence on August 13, 1802, that he presented this dissertation. For his final examination in theory at the Caroline Academy of Law he delivered, this same year, his dissertation on the 14th Law of Toro.

In the dissertation on the Indians, his ideas were, as usual, constructive and clothed in diplomatic language. He says that the laws themselves forbid the Indians' having to carry on their backs,[9] out of the mines, the heavy loads of metal as well as their tools, and that he knows that it would be more valuable to Spain to take better care of the Indians who, under present conditions, were dying off at such a rate that a fourth of each shift which worked a mine was lost. It is better, he insists, "to conserve the life of mortals than that of metals!" [10] (The name of Victorian de Villava, reformer and prosecuting attorney for the High Court of Charcas, who had also upheld the rights of the Indians in his *Discurso Sobre La Mita*, is cited twice. Villava, who died this same year, 1802, was a precursor of much of Moreno's innovative reasoning.) To highlight his description of how hard the work in the mines could be, Mariano quoted Pliny and Seneca and even Plautus, all of whom, he says, had compared digging in the mines to the sufferings of hell.

There is no hint here, or elsewhere, in Mariano's early writings that he would consent to use violence to uproot the old evils. Yet violent methods were often discussed by the group which surrounded his friend, the priest Francisco Medina. Later we shall see Medina, himself, enter the armed revolt in Chuquisaca in 1809, which predated, of course, the revolutionary occurrences in Buenos Aires. Although Mariano did not agree with such headlong measures as the 1809 revolt, his first act upon learning that he was to be secretary of the revolutionary Junta of Buenos Aires in 1810 was a characteristic act of loyalty to his friend. He demanded that the Viceroy sign a release for Medina from the prison where he had been thrown by the royalist troops sent to crush the uprising.

While Mariano was at the university, Chuquisaca counted little over 13,000 inhabitants, about half the size of Buenos Aires at this time.[11] Its Court and its Archbishopric were much older, however, than similar institutions in the port city, and the atmosphere of Spanish tradition and sharply drawn lines between classes were accordingly greater. There was, besides, the constant spectacle of mistreated Indians passing through the streets on their way to the mines. Mariano was so touched by their wretched aspect that he made a special trip to the silver mines of Potosí to examine the cruel conditions under which the Spanish Governor there, Paula Sanz, allowed them to be worked. It was this trip together with the causes of the Indian uprising years before under Tupac–Amaru and the horrors of its repression (Tupac's body having been torn apart by being tied to horses ridden in four different directions) which inspired his dissertation exposing the misapplication of the laws and the Indians' hopeless plight.

In contrast to the mournful procession of mitayos (Indian miners) there stood out the picturesque setting of

Chuquisaca. Its inland location on a valley plateau surrounded by the foothills of the Andes gave a touch of drama, a hemmed in, lid-on-the-cauldron aspect to all controversies. This remote situation also lent the individual a rather intense consciousness of himself, making him "extreme in haughtiness, if he were an official, advanced in humility and despair if he were a poor Indian, and consumed with hidden revolt if he were a university student of modest creole circumstances," who was sure to experience the greatest difficulty in finding a good job after he left college.

Such were the characteristics typical of a town that was one of the oldest settlements of the Spaniards in South America. It had been founded on an Inca village, in a district which was the last conquest the Incas had added to their empire when they were vanquished by the Spaniards. Early on, its situation near the rich mining center of Potosí created its chief attraction. Then as time passed, because of its better climate and natural beauty, Chuquisaca became the preferred residence of most of the miners who exploited the Potosí silver. The historian René-Moreno tells us that in the eighteenth century the city was one of the richest in all Latin America, due to the fact that the wealthy mine owners from the surrounding districts came to spend the last third of their lives there.

Upon Mariano's arrival in the year 1800 the relationship of Chuquisaca's government to that of Buenos Aires had already undergone a definite change from its earlier status. In the old days, before the elevation of the Provinces of the Río de La Plata into a Viceroyalty, the high judge of the Court of Charcas located in Chuquisaca had held supreme authority over all the provinces of the southern part of Spanish America, with the exception of the Captaincy General of Chile.[12] At the time the head of this Court, or *Audiencia*, was called a President, and the district of Charcas over which he ruled, a *Presidencia*. This name was also applied to the districts underneath the jurisdiction of the Courts at Guadalajara and Quito. One may ask why the title of President, which had an oddly republican sound in those days of Spanish Empire, was a title given only to the magistrate presiding over high courts not located at the capitals of Viceroyalties or Captaincies General. The answer sounds paradoxical, since *Presidencia* was a distinguishing term for a region where the Court held political as well as judicial authority—the opposite of that connected today with countries in which presidents are elected to hold executive duties only.

Thus we see that before 1777 (the date of the Viceroyalty of La Plata) the President of Charcas — although subject to supervision by the Viceroy in Lima—was practically a supreme ruler. In judicial matters his court was the last word for a vast district, the only appeal from its decisions being to the Council of the Indies in Spain. But after the erection of the Viceroyalty of the Río de La Plata, the Court of Charcas was compelled to divide its jurisdiction with the Court of Buenos Aires, retaining its exclusive power only over La Paz, Cochabamba, and Potosí. At the same time an advance in the division of powers in these regions occurred with the curtailment of the court's authority, which had once included administrative and executive powers too, to strictly judicial matters. The departments of police, treasury, and war went first to the Viceroy of the Río de La Plata, of which Charcas or Upper Peru (as it was often called) had become a part, and later to the heads (Gobernadores Intendentes) of the four intendencies into which this section of the Viceroyalty was divided in 1782.

Chuquisaca, as we know, was famous not only for its Court, but also for being the residence of the Archbishop and center of the archbishopric of Charcas. Paradoxically there was less serious religion here than in Buenos Aires. Most of the clergy, with the exception of the saintly Archbishop, conducted themselves more like men of the world than like ministers of the church. Even their clothes were ostentatious, and in all places they were the soul of society and pleasure. Many of them, who had come into the city from outlying parishes in the barren desert or mountains, would spend all their savings in diversion and gambling.

On the whole the atmosphere would have seemed almost glittering to Mariano, especially with the university life to give it added zest. As we have noted, it was the University of San Francisco Xavier, second only to the University of San Marcos in Lima, for which the city was most famous. At the time of graduation, when all the leading families held open house for the graduates, there occurred giddy processions of students throughout the town. The students would divide into bands and go singing with their guitars down the streets, and young girls would lean from their balconies and throw garlands of flowers around their necks. It may have been on one of these occasions that Mariano first saw Maria Guadalupe Cuenca, whom he was to marry two years later. Although he did not usually join the student processions or escapades, he surely did so on the great day of receiving his university diploma.

At least we can hope that the frivolous side of the city's life claimed him at times during this university interlude. Certainly there is no other period in his life when he seems to have done much else but work and struggle, first to support his family and later to "form the men" and the nation for which Fray Cayetano had prepared him. According to stories told the author by his descendants, in Chuquisaca he did find himself, for once, engaged in scenes that were both dramatic and romantic.

One such occasion occured on the day he had just finished his apprenticeship in the law office of Dr. Estevan Agustín Gascon. It was a summer day, late in February, 1804, and he was leaving the *Audiencia* with his law license in his pocket. Now, at last, after two years of study and two years of apprenticeship, he was *licenciado*. His examiners had said of his response to their questions that he showed not only great talent and aptitude for the law, but that he had proved himself to be the type of student who brought most brilliance and renown to the Academy which had prepared him.

He was wondering what his parents would say when they heard. Walking on through the streets, he thought of the tenderness with which his mother had cared for him during the time he was sick with smallpox, of the gift of her jewels — her only luxury — when he left Buenos Aires. He remembered how she, especially, wanted him to enter the church. A desire to see and talk to her, to tell her of the Canon's approval of his legal preparation, of the excitement he had found in the ideas of Rousseau and the Encyclopedists, of the need he felt to raise the creoles to positions of equality with the Spaniards, to self-government — all these thoughts rushed headlong. He wanted to go home at once and take his mother a present. The impulse, the beauty of the day, the exultation of his examiners' words caused him to stop in front of the window of a shop where trinkets and works of art were sold.

At once his eye was caught by a miniature, painted by a well known artist of the town.[14] From the frame there shone forth the face of a young girl whose expression reminded him, perhaps, of the mother whose memory was at that moment so compelling. Who had sat for this portrait? Would it be possible to meet her? More possible, surely, than the long trip back home.

"It's a very young girl, scarcely fourteen," the shopkeeper said. "Maria, daughter of the widow Guadalupe Cuenca."

Had there been a double recognition? Could he have seen in the painting both a resemblance to one of the young girls who threw garlands to the graduates as well as to his mother? Such a serene, warm, and yet exalted expression in those eyes. Not a beautiful face in the ordinary way, but lovely because of the reflection of an interior, moral force. He learned that Maria was a student at the *Convent of the Monjas Buenas*. He did not leave the shop until he had purchased the miniature.

Summer, and autumn on the way. Marriage? The priesthood would have denied him marriage. But now he was a lawyer. The die was cast.

He took the small painting to the Canon Terrazas and told him of his desire to meet the young girl. The Canon, who knew her family, approved. That Sunday, Mariano (according to Julian Delfin Martino's version of the family legend) saw Maria in the procession of Convent students on their way to Mass. The girl of the miniature — headlong love! .... Was it possible? But in a few days he would be opening his own law office, receiving clients, making enough to support a wife, if all went well. His heart, after its long restraint, leapt forward to marriage, just as, later, it would leap toward independence for his people. Maria felt his glance, his ardor. This boy whose intense eyes sought hers, who was he? She could not wait to know. Then she remembered — the protegé of the powerful Canon.

When the Canon and Mariano came to call that afternoon, both the widow and her daughter were prepared. Either then, or soon afterwards, Mariano asked for Maria's hand in marriage and her mother consented. The engagement did not last long. As was the custom, Mariano courted his fiancée only in her home in the presence of her family, but

there may have been chance meetings, properly chaperoned, elsewhere in the comparatively small town.

There were many plazas and squares where he could
walk in the hopes of catching a glimpse of Maria as she went
on some errand, accompanied by a nun of the convent
where she went to school. In particular there was a small
square called the *Glorieta*, situated at the end of the
Avenida Prado, and graced with carved benches surrounding a central fountain. The *Glorieta*, besides, was planted
with beds of white lilies and red roses, and was shaded from
the afternoon sun by trees such as the eucalyptus and
chirimoya. What better setting for a lovers' tryst?

When Mariano did not see his sweetheart here, she,
chaperoned by an older relative or one of the sisters from
the convent, found occasion to be in the *Plaza Mayor* if she
knew it was a day when he had gone for research in the
library of the university and would soon be leaving the gates
which opened on to the huge square. But if one of the judges
of the Court happened to be passing by, the couple would be
out of luck if Mariano failed to notice. For any man who did
not flourish a sweeping bow with his hat as a judge passed
by in his calash was guilty of contempt of court. In fact, he
must not only bow, but follow and escort the judge to his
residence. And if anyone were unfortunate enough to be on
horseback when a judge passed him on foot, that person—
should he fail to dismount in deference to His Honor—might
easily be imprisoned or fined.[15]

Certainly Mariano was not apt to forget any of the
amenities of conduct. And he was especially careful to
observe them when he was with Maria. His only daring with
her was to marry her secretly, with the Canon's approba-
tion. And his only indiscretions, if they can be so called,
were in the biting truths of his briefs. Later on in Chuquisaca these truths would get him into trouble.

(One wonders if he may ever have gone with his wife's family to one of the bullfights which were so much more colorful in Chuquisaca than in Buenos Aires. René-Moreno describes the way special *corridas* were celebrated with *toros de cuerda*, which meant that there was no pen for the bulls but that they were brought into the ring by peons who dragged them on ropes through the streets and *plazuelas*, exciting and frightening everybody en route. However, as bullfights were frowned on by the clergy in Buenos Aires, it is unlikely that Mariano attended them in Chuquisaca unless in a spirit of adventure with his university friends.)

His secret marriage to Maria was more of a challenge to his parents than to anyone else. Mariano had kept the marriage secret, at first, because he did not wish the elder Morenos to worry about how he would support a wife. Evidently, as soon as he opened his own law office and was bringing in more income, he wrote his family about her. He told them of her sweetness and beauty and innocence. Of how she was only fourteen when they married and had been educated, up until a year before their wedding, in a convent.

At first the elder Morenos were disheartened by the marriage of this son whom they had always visualized in the robes of a priest. Had he not, after graduating as Bachelor in Theology, requested and received the dimissory letters for the tonsure and for minor orders?[16] Had he not, in a letter to Fray Cayetano, asked the friar to persuade his father to petition the Viceroy for an exemption from the fee usually paid for a degree of Doctor in Theology? Don Manuel, swallowing his Spanish pride, had obtained the exemption. And now . . . all for nothing! What had come over the boy?

True, he had graduated in Civil Law, too, that same year. His thirst for knowledge, the friar had explained. . . . Remember, even as a youngster, he had needled them, with his importunity to learn, to go to a university. That time, for instance, that he had asked his father, "If there's not enough money, why don't you sell your gold buckles?" The very buckles worn on shoes for dress occasions for a *besa manos* or a Viceregal reception. Those Mariano would have sacrificed, those buckles of an ex-member of the Boundary Commission appointed to settle the line between the colonies of Spain and Portugal — the high point of Don Manuel's career. His father had answered Mariano standing there before him—flushed and with eyes shining— *"No, por Dios, esos bucles son nuestra decencia!"* [17] They were the family sign of honor, of decency. "I was firm with him, then," the father groaned. "Perhaps we should have been firmer still!"

The friar thought otherwise, and perhaps also Ana Maria, Mariano's mother, remembering how she had forced on him the day he left for Chuquisaca her small luxury of jewels. What hurt his parents the most was that Mariano had not written first of his intention to marry. If his mother could only have known something of the girl, of this Maria Guadalupe Cuenca. And yet Fray Cayetano had said that he was not too surprised. Let Mariano come home, then, let him come home so that they, too, could know his wife.

In a recently published collection of letters the anxiety the young lawyer felt about how the news of his marriage would be received is reflected in Fray Cayetano's answer to a letter from Mariano written June 15, 1804. The friar wrote,

> Why did you expect my anger [about your marriage]? Did you think I was unyielding about the opposite course for you? I didn't expect this one so soon, true; but if you thought it right to advance the date of your marriage, then, well and good, and even more, if, as you say, it has had such an effect on you for the better. What do you wish now? A blessing, poorer than that already given you by the curate?.... If any more blessings can

come to you, let them be showered both on you and your **good companion,** Doña Maria Cuenca, whom I salute with the greatest affection, wishing to serve and please her with the same ardor, love and *cariño* that I feel for Mariano. So much for my anger!

I have been with your parents, they shed a few tears, they resented that you did it without their previous consent. I consoled them, I brought them around. In your letters you will see they are mollified. They would have preferred to see you a priest. But parents can't make all the decisions for their sons. But they begged me that, in the same way I'd been go-between to soften their attitude toward you, I'd also mediate with you so they could have the joy of seeing you here with your wife as soon as possible.

You ask me if you can make a good enough living here to support her. *Hijo mío,* here in your capacity you won't get rich because there are many [lawyers], but you will make enough to live. . . . Resources aren't lacking, you're young. . .come, my dear Mariano. . .you'll have a house to live in, a family to console, friends who want you here, and a poor friar who, in the midst of his nothing, finds himself with everything with the sole thought of seeing you in his cell and giving you a strong embrace with all the affection of his heart. When I tell you this there strike within me a thousand thoughts and there come to my eyes a few tears which make me know that I have been loving Mariano more than he could ever guess. . . . [18]

Later, in September, a year before Mariano's return to Buenos Aires, another letter of the friar's reflects still further Mariano's anxiety to make a better living. The friar counsels him against applying for a position that would necessitate influence with higher officials and keep him from returning home. All the same, Brother Cayetano, who could refuse him nothing, consents to help with the "higher officials." [19]

With the publication of these letters in the book on
Moreno by Roman Francisco Pardo we are given a graphic
picture of the struggle that was going on within the future
revolutionary to conform and provide for his family under a
system where it was almost impossible for a young,
educated creole, who did not know how to work with his
hands, to live without influence. Here, indeed, reflected in
the answers to his own letters, is a Moreno of Spanish sensitivity and pride, of gentleness and conservatism — strong
tendencies planted early by his parents. The other strain —
the compulsion to lay bare the inequities of the system, to
risk his livelihood by exposing corruption — is also present.

Before his marriage, while preparing himself in law and
precedent at the Caroline Academy (the law school of the
University), he had also participated in the give and take of
argument at the informal meetings of students after hours.
There was much to discuss. Chuquisaca was a veritable
hotbed of invective. Everyone from lawyers and curates
and shopkeepers down to the clerks and assistant clerks
and slaves would enter harangues about the latest directive
of a new archbishop, or the most recent silver mine conces-
sion, or the description of the worldly goods of some recent
visitor to the town. But the university graduates discussed
more serious matters.

Even as a practising lawyer, Moreno continued to meet
with his former fellow students. The favorite topic of the
leader of the group, the priest Medina, was the scornful
wording of Royal Cedulas. To Francisco Medina it was
disgraceful that the Spanish monarch could annul the most
solemn laws in such an arbitrary manner as to say, "I
declare such a law null and void because it is my will."

"He does not say," Medina would declare, " 'because
this is just, because it is necessary, nor even because I
believe it and it is convenient for me.' What he says, in fact,

is 'I order what is contrary to the laws because I want to, because this is my fancy, because such is my will!' " This so incensed the priest from La Paz that he usually ended his speech by crying out, "The hour for reform is ready to strike and the revolution draws near!" [20]

Mariano would come away inspired. He would come away remembering how Fray Cayetano had written, "It disgusts me to grease the palms of scamps," [21] "but I'll help you become a subdelegate if you wish." He no longer wished.

While the others contented themselves by talking rather vaguely of revolution, Mariano dared to risk his position, even after his marriage to Maria, by defending a man who had incurred the enmity of one of the all-powerful judges. His former patron, the Canon Terrazas, advised him that it would be healthier for him to leave Chuquisaca after this case. He had better take his wife and child and depart, before he could be arrested.

Thus we find him, over a year after his marriage, on his way back home to Buenos Aires. In September, 1805, at long last, he returned to the city where he was born.

V

The Lawyer in Buenos Aires During the English Invasions, 1806, 1807

"The Plaza had a thousand means of defense, and 500 of our men would have been enough to rout the enemy, who, having already landed on the coast, had taken a position from which they could not attack effectively; but we had the bad luck to be led by high officials who were as stupid in military matters as the Marqués," (Marqués de Sobremonte, Viceroy of Buenos Aires in 1806.) "Their absolute ignorance was such that, when they tried to sign a surrender they did not even know how to do it and had to make use of a merchant.

"I saw many men weep in the Plaza for the infamy with which we were delivered to the enemy; and I, myself, more than any other, felt the tears running down my cheeks when, at 3 o'clock the afternoon of June 27th, 1806, I saw 1,500 Englishmen enter the Plaza, who, having taken possession of my country, began locating themselves in the fort and other military quarters of the city."

—Moreno, Manuel, *Vida y Memorias del Dr. Don Mariano Moreno*, p. 85.

The man who was to write the above description in 1806 came home to Buenos Aires (almost a year before the invasion he recorded) in much better circumstances than he had been at the time of his departure for Chuquisaca, five years earlier. Traveling with his wife and eight-months-old son, Moreno entered the city in a private carriage, with a servant. The manner of his arrival shows how much, in spite of difficulties, he had been able to improve his livelihood by his own efforts in one short year of independent law practice.

The Buenos Aires that he came back to on that September day of 1805 had also undergone notable changes. According to Mariano's memoirs of the English invasions a year later, the population had grown from about 40,000 to 60,000. The most obvious change was the aspect of the *Plaza Mayor*. Before, wagons from the country had come in to sell their supplies haphazardly and butchers slaughtered their beeves wherever it was convenient, hanging the meat up on huge hooks protruding from their oxcarts. At the same time, broom sellers and poultry vendors, with cylindrical coops hanging from the ends of sticks slung across their shoulders, cried out their wares in a constant weaving back and forth between stacks of oranges and vegetables set up in any place their owners might choose. Today, the country village had become a city. There was actually an imposing sense of order and importance, for now most of the market vendors occupied their own private booths under the arches of a long corridor recently erected, called the *Recova*. This arched covering cut dramatically across the center of the Plaza.

Mariano asked the driver of his rented coach to drive through its central arch for the sake of pointing out to Maria something that did not exist in Chuquisaca—a plaza not only overlooking the river with the sea beyond, but a plaza big enough to support a covered market corridor, so

imposing that one could guide a coach or a wagon straight
through its central passageway. He must have explained to
his wife that this spacious Plaza was natural for a port,
handling such necessary products as hides and tallow. Products not as costly and luxurious as silver, but of much more
widespread and popular use in the world as a whole, *if* that
world could ever become a customer.

In spite of his pride in the city's development—so soon
to be wounded by the English invasions—he spared for the
Plaza only the time necessary to cross it. His chief excitement and concern lay in the prospect of seeing his family
again. Even faced with the anger of the judge, which his last
case had incited, he might have stayed on in Chuquisaca except for the fact that he wanted to come home to console his
parents.[1] His father's health, he sensed, was failing. All the
more reason that he should establish himself quickly.

Soon after his arrival he applied for the authorization
necessary for his practice of the law in Buenos Aires.[2] A few
days later we find him with a client.

It is interesting to note that the pattern of most of
Mariano's cases—the defense of a comparatively unpro-
tected client against the abuse of some established custom
or high authority—was marked out from the beginning with
this first case that he took in Buenos Aires. Had a reputation for daring and brilliance preceded him?

His client was one of his former teachers at San Carlos,
the Canon Don Melchior Frenandez. Fernandez, in the exercise of his functions as Magistral Canon, had taken the
side of his congregation against a host of vexations and
petty reforms instituted by the Spanish Bishop Lué. (We
shall meet this haughty bishop later, speaking in Open
Cabildo meeting against self-government for Buenos
Aires.)

By the time Mariano arrived in the city, the controversies between the Bishop and his canons, representing the various churches, had reached a climax. Bishop Lué had already started prosecution of Fernandez, his principal opponent, in the Ecclesiastical Court. Knowing how arbitrary the Ecclesiastical Court would be in favoring a Spaniard and a bishop, the public was awaiting the outcome with apprehension and little hope. Mariano knew this of course. He tried an innovative tactic. Taking advantage of a law which allowed the matter to be transferred to the Civil Court, he took the case and won it, by the extraordinary recourse of "*de fuerza*" (as such transfers were called) before the *Audiencia*, the high court of Buenos Aires.

His triumph was not without its tragedy. The day he made his argument and won the case his father's health had begun to sink rapidly. He would die before the day was over.[3] Deaf to the applause with which the crowds in the plaza were greeting him, Mariano rushed from the courthouse to return to his father's bedside. Once again the scene is a dramatic forewarning of the many occasions, mixed of triumph and sorrow, which stand out in his life.

Shortly after the winning of his case he was named one of the two *relators* of the High Court of Buenos Aires. Although the post of *relator* or counsellor was a subordinate one, it entailed important work. The main duty of the *relator* was to look up references and help prepare opinions for the judges. At the same time, the *relator* was allowed to take private cases of his own.

It was not long after Moreno's appointment that the English started to invade the city, in June of 1806. As noted in the record he kept of those days, their attack was completely unprepared for. Yet the British occupation lasted scarcely six weeks. On August 12, the amazing reconquest by the people took place.

The record Mariano kept of the invasion is contained in

the memoirs which he felt called upon to write when, in the days immediately following the fight for the city, he could no longer concentrate on his work at the court. Love of Buenos Aires and pride in its people—the ordinary, everyday, cross-section of people of all walks of life—who defended her shine through his memoirs. Buenos Aires had always staunchly stood her ground in the old days, he says. She had fought off invasions of the Querandíes, raids by pirates, encroachments by the Dutch and the French. Under a good commander she had even taken La Colonia de Sacramento from the Portuguese. It is "infamy" that she should have had to bow to the invader only because of the criminal carelessness and stupidity of her Viceroy.

Not once does Mariano use such vivid sarcasm against the invaders as he uses against the inept rulers of the colony. With each word of disgust for the rulers, who "did not even know how many canons they had until the English took them out of the warehouses," [4] there is an implied sympathy and pride for the *hijos del país*, the people. If only they had been commanded by real leaders instead of by cowards! "Our numerous and skillful cavalry would have pressed the enemy's rearguard, would have cut them off!" [5]

How revealing of Moreno's character are these memoirs, witness as they are to the mixture in him of scholar and democratic statesman, so different from the stereotype that we in the United States attach to most Latin American politicians. The pages of these *Memoirs* demonstrate how he alone, of all the victims of those days of foreign occupation, felt so urgently the need to analyze what was wrong that he had to pour into writing—not later but on the spot—the indignation as well as the great challenge he felt to change, someday, a criminally unfit government. We see this urge again in one of the phrases he liked best to quote—the admonition from Fénélon's *Telemachus* "to love your family better than yourself, your country better than your family, and humanity best of all." [6] More and more he was going to have to put this maxim to the test, as well as another that he quoted often from Raynal, who, in praising the English language, had written, "This language has been the first in which was said 'the majesty of the people'; this expression, alone, consecrates a language!" [7] While resisting their invasion (not sanctioned by the British government as it would turn out later) he did not let his resistance blind him to the good qualities of the English.

For him and for his country the disaster would later turn into a benefit with the *Reconquista*. As we shall see, the two British invasions are prelude to Moreno's service to his people in work for both the Cabildo and the Court. And yet this work was doubly hard for him at first, with his heart heavy over the loss of his father.

His father, he reflected, had done so much to help him. Now more than ever he appreciated how Don Manuel had aided his Degree in Theology by procuring for him an exemption, from the Viceroy del Pino, of the usual fee that had to be paid. Asking a favor, which was so repugnant to the elder Moreno, was something he would never have done for himself, Mariano knew. So it is that he felt reluctant, at first, to take on any extra duties which would further prevent him from giving that intimate and detailed attention to his mother which his father wished. But the invasions changed this situation, and he soon offered his services to the government.

Meanwhile, not only Mariano but other observers were wondering why the Spanish authorities could not have foreseen the invasion and prepared for it. Didn't everyone know that since 1795, when Spain had stepped out of the coalition against the French revolutionary armies, there had been hostility beteen Spain and England? And that the general peace of Amiens signed in 1802 had been of short duration, since in 1803 war was again declared between England and France. And didn't those in the government know that this same year Spain had exasperated England by buying from Napoleon, at the price of a huge subsidy, the right to remain neutral? [8] Not too long ago England had punished this defection of the Spanish king, Carlos IV, by seizing four Spanish frigates on their way home from the colonies. Later, in 1805, both the Spanish and the French navies, which had by then joined forces, were whipped by the British at Trafalgar on October 21.

Prior to these events there had been talk in England of lending aid to the colonies for a revolt from Spain. The roots of this intriguing idea could not be laid to the British so much as to a daring Venezuelan general, one Francisco Miranda, who, ever since 1790, had been working in Europe to procure military help for a colonial revolution. [9] And in 1804, after the capture of the Spanish frigates, it began to look as if the British would support Miranda. They promised that Sir Hume Popham would cooperate with him, in return for the opening of all Spanish American ports to British trade. The plan fell through, but Popham remembered it when he sailed under his government's orders to take the Dutch Cape of Good Hope. Although he had no orders to take Buenos Aires the prize must have seemed too tempting and too near to pass up. He decided on his own to make an attack.

How could the Viceroy have been surprised? The plots of Miranda were fairly well known, and one of the young creole hotheads of the day, Saturniño Rodríguez Peño, was even working in Buenos Aires as Miranda's agent. [10] But while it may have been natural to overlook the adventurous and impractical scheming of a group of young men, the seizure of the Spanish frigates bearing colonial goods, to say nothing of the defeat at Trafalgar, should have put the government on the alert. Even more alarming should have been the notice of the British capture of the Cape of Good Hope.

Yet, upon hearing this news, what did the Viceroy Sobremonte do? He promptly dispatched all the veteran troops of Buenos Aires, including the last regiment of Spanish dragoons, to Montevideo.[11] When the British disembarked at Quilmes on June 25, the capital of the Viceroyalty was practically defenseless, even after an adjutant had brought Sobremonte the news the evening before, while he was enjoying himself at the theater.[12] A few hours after the landing of the British soldiers, the Viceroy fled to Córdoba with his family. And on June 27 the British, under General Beresford, took possession of the city.

The occupation, or "possession," was only external, however, in spite of the lenient conditions of their rule and their promise of free trade.[13] From the very beginning the populace started hatching plans for the reconquest of the city, and the British must have read these plans on the faces of the people everywhere. General Beresford tried to make himself as agreeable as possible, of course. Some families, such as the Sarrateas, geared themseleves up to entertain and cater to his officers. Meanwhile, young zealots were plotting to explode mines under the fortress where the British General was living.[14]

Blow up the Viceregal fortress? Wasn't there a better way? The patriots were discussing other schemes. For instance, the young Martín de Pueyrredón had hatched an ambitious plan. A creole youth of wealthy family who had been educated abroad, Pueyrredón began equipping at his own expense a thousand men both from the city and from the outskirts—anyone who could ride a horse.[15] There were gauchos among them. In fact this spontaneous cavalry was to form an inspiration later for Mariano's democratic rules governing the armies of the independence. Pueyrredón's troops, however, did not meet with success. His little company, which had never fought before, was no match for the disciplined British troops, whom they attacked four miles away from Buenos Aires, on the fields of Perdriel. The young patriots were quickly routed.

The honor of rescuing Buenos Aires would go, instead, to an intriguing foreigner with years of military experience behind him. This new leader was Santiago Liniers, a Frenchman by birth but an employee of the Spanish government, who was serving as Captain in the port of Ensenada. How could the patriots arrange for him to come to Buenos Aires? They did so by means of a safe conduct obtained through an Irishman named O'Gorman.

Captain Liniers entered the city and took a good look at the strength of the British troops. Satisfied and excited by what he had seen, Liniers was able to slip out of the occupied city soon afterwards to Montevideo, and to borrow troops from the Spanish Governor there for a landing on the opposite coast and a march on Buenos Aires. While some of Pueyrredón's troops joined these forces, other creole regiments marched on Buenos Aires from another direction. Between them, on August 12, they recaptured the city.[16] Day of glory, day of ecstasy! The British had ruled only forty-six days.

Yet wait. Don't be too sure that we are safe. The invaders are going to try to regain their lost prize. So argued the people, after their first wave of triumph. We had better prepare and lose no time about it.

Not yet willing to leave their fate entirely in the hands of Liniers, they decided to prepare for the next crisis by making their voices heard on August 14 in what was known as an Open Cabildo meeting. Open Cabildo meant that the Cabildo proper, in an emergency, could issue invitations to people outside its ranks (members of the Court, lawyers, clerks, merchants, creole landholders) to join in its deliberations. No later than two days after their ousting of the British they decided in their town council meeting to relieve the Viceroy Sobremonte of his command in Buenos Aires, while at the same time allowing him to rule in the rest of the Viceroyalty.[17] In the capital they elevated Captain Liniers to temporary command of the troops in Sobremonte's place, with the court ruling in civil matters until another Viceroy could be named.

Mariano Moreno, waiting at first in the Plaza and then later entering the building, will make mental notes of this meeting, where, for the first time, the creoles literally shouted their defiance of Spain. Here is what happened.

The Spanish residents, determined to take the lead on this occasion, had prevailed on their friends in the Cabildo to limit the meeting at first to a session confined mostly to judges and high officials.[18] While the session was taking place behind the closed doors of the council chamber on the second floor of the Cabildo building, something else happened. The interested populace had come in crowds to the Plaza. Water sellers, broom boys, proprietors and waiters from the two popular cafes of Mallco and Los Catalanes, gaucho soldiers from Pueyrredón's and Liniers' armies, to say nothing of the alert creole youths who plotted insurrection, such as Antonio Berutti, Domingo French, Tomas Guido, the Rodríguez Peñas, Manuel Belgrano and others— all these people milled back and forth below the Cabildo porch, restless, inquisitive, feeling they who had helped fight for the city had been left out.

Somewhere in the crowd, along with his brother Manuel, Mariano (not yet reinstated as *relator*) stood waiting and watching the faces of the others, studying and gauging their reactions. All at once a rumor circulates that the session is deciding to erect a Junta to govern Buenos Aires, with the discredited Sobremonte at its head.

But this is impossible! The people begin to jeer. They shout oaths against the coward who had deserted them. Then one of the Spanish lawyers at the meeting, a certain Badillo, supposedly a relative of one of Minister Godoy's majordomos, conceives a brilliant piece of strategy.

"Let me walk out and quiet them by parading the banner with the king's portrait," he suggests. In a few minutes, followed by a procession of thirty or more "big wigs," Badillo walks out on the balcony with his gold and crimson banner and marches up and down.

Unimpressed, the populace begins to laugh and make jokes. It was by their own efforts, without any help from the Viceroy who had fled, that they had driven a foreign invader from the city. Who is this silly Spaniard, anyway? Parading the portrait of the king—what is he trying to do? To humble them!

Just who does he think they are? Doesn't he realize that notices come to them in foreign ships of the disgraceful happenings at the Spanish court? Of how Minister Godoy is the Queen's lover, of how Godoy, himself, is probably responsible for the weak state of Spain, a nation in which Napoleon dictates policy? Isn't the Spanish court responsible for sending them such inept and cowardly officials as Sobremonte? If Badillo thinks they do not know these things they will show him.

They begin to scream forth insults.

"Throw out Godoy!"

"Hang him on the gallows!"

"Yes, and string up Doña Maria Louisa in the middle to make him tender!" [19]

Badillo and his men rush for cover. The people crash through the doors of the meeting. Their leaders demand that Liniers be made their commander-in-chief. They also demand that the *Audiencia* become the political executive until Spain could either name Liniers as Viceroy or send a new one. The Cabildo, they agree, can be in charge of raising and equipping an army for defense.[20]

In the next few days, with this new provisional government in command, Mariano was asked to take up again his post of *relator* of the Court.

But it was more than the work of *relator* that was facing him now. His position of trust in connection with the Court, united to his reputation as a defender of the peoples' rights (gained in the Fernandez case), marked him at once as being of special use in this period of transition from an absolute Spanish rule. Thus it was natural that the Cabildo, with its many new duties to perform, relative to the maintenance of an army, called on him for help in the issuance of its proclamations. He now begins to fill, in addition to his duties at the Court, the position of *assessor* or legal adviser for the Town Council.

He began by advising the municipal body about expenditures and the execution of plans for the payment of salaries to primary teachers, as well as to officers and troops. Other outstanding examples of his advice included directions on advances made to the *Royal Hacienda* for the purpose of freeing negro slaves who had fought in the Reconquest, plans for pensions to widows and invalids, endowments to orphans, and construction of bridges and corrals of supply. At the same time he managed to persuade the Court to change a sentence from death to imprisonment for a client of his, named Capello, who had been seen talking with the British when they were masters of the city. He pointed out that Capello, who could speak English, was trying to persuade the British to hand over some land he had bought and been prevented from taking over under Sobremonte, because such possession interfered with the illegal use that a powerful Spaniard had been making of it.[21] Although Mariano could not prevent his client's being thrown into prison, Capello's release was one of the first acts he performed on the eve of the revolution of 1810.

During the days between the two English invasions the double load of his duties caused him to turn down most of the invitations he and Maria received. According to his brother, Manuel, he refused "the most obliging invitations which he frequently received for outings and other diversions so that he could dedicate himself entirely to his work, to the care of his family and to his study. All his pleasures were reduced to these things. The satisfaction that he found in using his time in this way compensated him for the fatigue which would have seemed insupportable to anyone else." [22]

The fatigue was caused not only by work but by the need to economize. On December 4, 1807, he directed a memorial to King Carlos IV asking for an appointment as *Assesor* (Legal Counsellor) in one of the Intendencies of the Viceroyalty. He stated that he was almost "without resources" to provide for his widowed mother and for the education of his eight younger brothers.[23] When this request was denied Mariano seems to have survived the refusal by practising even greater economy.

It is notable that neither his heavy load of work nor his precarious financial condition turned him into a sour individual, much less into either a subversive or "communist radical" type, a label which certain leftist historians would like to claim for him today. His deep religious faith, love of family and sense of humor protected him against any such self-seeking extremism. For he had "a happy disposition," his brother tells us, "with nothing frivolous in it. His jokes were very ingenious and never directed to low or indecent objects. This made his society delightful, and his friends coveted his conversation and were amused by his sallies." [24]

During the time Moreno was busy wording the Cabildo's local proclamations, the Town Council was communicating with young Pueyrredón, whom it had sent as its agent to Spain. The chief reason for this mission lay in the fact that Don Martín Alzaga, who was now the principal *Alcalde*, was jealous of Liniers' authority and wanted more power to be given to the Cabildo. Pueyrredón was even told to ask permission for the Cabildo to make protests against any carelessness of which a Viceroy might be guilty. In other words, the Cabildo wished to be guardian of the rights of the colony. The fact was that many of the new troops were already totally dependent for their salaries on the pocketbook of the Alcalde Alzaga.

Because of this dependence Moreno had to exercise a careful balance of diplomacy between the execution of commissions for the Cabildo and his duties at the Court. He knew that all the judges, as well as most of the new troops who were called *Patricios*, composed entirely of creoles— troops whom Liniers had put under the command of Don Cornelio Saavedra — were in favor of making the French hero of the Reconquest at least temporary Viceroy. But there was something about Liniers that Mariano distrusted. In the sessions of the Court, for instance, he was in a position to know the wording of messages sent by Liniers to Napoleon, which were full of flattery and of praise for the part certain French soliders would take in the defense of Montevideo later. Mariano did not like Liniers' levity nor his tone.[25]

But these considerations were subordinate to the need of defending the city against a second invasion by the

British. Moreno was apprehensive since he knew of the secret capitulation Liniers had signed for General Beresford for the Britisher to use to save face before the London Court. In this private document, Liniers promised to give up the British prisoners, although Beresford had surrendered unconditionally. And now in February of 1807, when news came that Montevideo had just fallen to a second attack by the British, whose army had been strengthened by reinforcements, this secret capitulation looked worse than ever. Sir Samuel Achmuty, now in power in Montevideo, demanded that Beresford himself be released in accordance with this paper.

The people in Buenos Aires, alerted to this request, became more and more suspicious. Release of Beresford could be dangerous, for he could give the British in Montevideo valuable information about the new bullet and sword factory, the new military school and the batteries recently built in the city. On February 10 the people called for a second *Cabildo Abierto*. This time the meeting demanded the recall of Sobremonte (who had been left in command over all the Viceroyalty except Buenos Aires). Well and good, Moreno thought. But when they asked for Liniers to be designated Viceroy in his place he began to worry about the consequences.

Moreno had spent little time during these days in taking cases on his own. From now on he was to have even less time. Yet it is noteworthy to observe that one of the cases which he did take was a suit to defend the Regiment of *Pardos* (colored men) against a proposed reduction in salary. He argued that the *Pardos* had given up positions and businesses that paid better than the army in order to enter the service, and that if their salaries were reduced they would not be able to provide for their families.[26] Since they had voluntarily taken up arms to defend the city, they should not have their pay reduced to that of the Provincial Militia, as was proposed. He noted that the Militia received other compensation, such as free uniforms, etc., which made their lower salary acceptable. But the *Pardos* had volunteered and made sacrifices, just as all the other new regiments had done, and yet they were the only regiment whose pay it was proposed to reduce. What crime had they committed, Moreno asks. Dramatically he emphasizes that the *Pardos* had been no less worthy than any other regiment in matters of obedience and patriotism. He won the case. Another in the pattern of his defense of the weak against the strong.

Now with the growing menace of the British from Montevideo, he directed most of his attention to the city's defense. Only a few days after his case for the Regiment of *Pardos*, the British again invaded Buenos Aires. The date was June 28, 1807. Winter again. A year since the first invasion. What did Liniers do? When he found the invaders had chosen a place different from their first landing, he was taken by surprise. Confused, he divided his troops, leaving half his men at Barracas and rushing forward with the others to cut off the British at Miserere. He was completely routed.

Under orders from the Cabildo, doubtless worded in part by Moreno, the citizens, themselves, together with other detachments of creole troops under Colonel Saavedra, saved the day. Aroused, fiercely proud, they determined to die rather than give in. For days volunteers from every walk of life had been digging fortifications around the *Plaza Mayor* — a plan initiated by the engineer Cerviño in conjunction with Alzaga. When the British troops started marching toward the Plaza, even women joined the citizen army to bar their way. Everywhere they manned the tops of the flat-roofed houses. The men fired the guns while women doused the invaders with burning hot oil from jars which they kept refilling.

At last Liniers returned to the Plaza in time to help them. On July 5, the British, having been repulsed by creole troops stationed in the chapels and monasteries of Santo Domingo, San Miguel, and La Merced, surrendered their arms. Not the Spanish garrison, but the *hijos del pais* — the American volunteer soldiers — had won the day.

After this victory, Mariano settled down once more to his work with the Court and the Cabildo. From now on we find him more than ever suspicious of Liniers.

VI

Growth of Moreno's Legal Reputation—Cases in Defense of The Oppressed

"Among the various effects of the English invasions, that of awakening the American class, of calling it into action and giving it the realization of its own valor, stands out. In 1807... the different political parties which will dispute the stage up until the moment of the revolution begin to take form: on one side are grouped most of the creoles, on the other, the peninsular Spaniards.... The Spanish party in 1808 combined its action with that of Montevideo, in order to realize a subversive movement for overthrowing the Viceroy and seizing all the official positions. In Montevideo, Governor Elío, in league with the Spaniards of Buenos Aires, rings the alert for action by calling a Cabildo Abierto and erecting, through it, a Junta in imitation of those which were being set up in the Peninsula. Both he and it (Elío and the Junta) refused recognition to Liniers. It was not possible to bring about a simultaneous coup in Buenos Aires; its authors were obliged to postpone their plans until January 1, 1809... in order to take advantage of the reelection of the members of the Municipality (Cabildo.)

"The outcome of this revolt was adverse to the

*Spanish party in the Capital. The
Viceroy. . . directed by creoles and most of the
military corps, at whose head was Saavedra, stood
out as the victor in that bloodless and agitated
contest of one day. . . .*

   *"Moreno took part in these events and was
apparently with the Spanish party.". . . . He "was
an enemy of Liniers and an adversary of his
government; he had always been. His opposition
was older than any political party. Liniers, man of
the world, affable, gallant . . . full of the military
glory acquired in the battles against the English,
was at the same time light, dissipated,
indecisive. . . lacking in the qualities necessary for a
good governor. . . . Besides, Liniers admired
Napoleon, prided himself on belonging to a country
governed 'wisely and gloriously' by the Emperor,
and committed the imprudence of directing to him
two official communiques, narrating his victories in
the campaigns against the English" (intimating in
one that the creoles' victory had been inspired by
admiration for the European dictator's
prowess.). . . . "Nothing more was needed for
Liniers' enemies to accuse him of being. . . a
traitor. . . . Moreno, like the others, and even more
than the others, because of his ardent nature, could
believe. . . in Liniers' infidelity; but whether he
believed in it or not, the facts. . . could have given
him doubts. . . . Moreno, in intervening as he did in
the events of January 1, 1809, obeyed motives of
internal politics. . . and did not feel the chains of
the colonies' dependence on Spain except to oppose
their transfer to a new ruler. In the hypothesis that
he could have thought of those chains and in the
possible emancipation of the Colony. . . it would not
be difficult to establish that his conduct could not
prejudice this tendency and that, on the contrary,
the deeds realized by the Spanish party, with the
object of . . . perpetuating the colony's power and*

influence, weakened the ties." . . . *"his [Moreno's]*
attitude and the circumstance of his being advisor
of the Court and counsellor of the Cabildo at the
same time, did not place him in an
equivocal. . .position. Ambiguity in conduct did not
coincide with his virile, consistent and resolute
character. Because he was a convinced opponent of
Liniers' government and a man without fear, the
post of relator *did not shackle his independence of*
judgement and action."

—Piñero, Norberto, *Escritos Politicos y*
Económicos de Moreno Prologo, pp. 14, 15, 16, 17.

Buenos Aires, released at last from the invader, made
the same plunge into a feverish atmosphere of relief that
characterizes most cities suddenly rescued from foreign
occupation. This plunge was a tremendous change for a colony that, until now, had been so docile under the top-heavy
suffocation of the Spanish rule.

Plots and counter plots, so dear to the Latin soul, now
take on new vigor. Once beneath the surface, they come out
into the open. The creoles, the "sons of the country," wax
enthusiastic one day over Liniers, and the next over Carlota
of Brazil. And all the while the local Spaniards were making
plans to grab the government for themselves.

In the midst of these plots the activities of Moreno
(experiencing at last a short period of respite from his most
pressing work) are almost an anomaly. Ever since their arrival in Buenos Aires with his dramatic first case for Fernandez followed by the death of his father, Mariano's wife,
Maria, had been telling herself that their child scarcely
knew him. Now for a few days father and son become father
and son. They went on walks through the city together, as
Mariano had done with his own father. Only this time it was

scenes of battles to fight back the invaders that they inspected. When the three-year-old grew tired, Mariano carried him piggy back.

"Take me to see Brother Cayetano's fort!" the child asked one day.

His father laughed. "You mean the monastery? *Como no!*"

So it was often that they visited the beloved friar and relived Mariano's school days.

"I expect you to grow up a leader, too," Fray Cayetano said to the child.

"Hooray!" Marianito cried. "A gaucho. A *caudillo*."

Cayetano smiled. "A statesman, *chico*. That *kind* of leader. A worker for free trade and free enterprise and government as the voice of the governed. Repeat after me —*por favor*."

When the child jumbled the words they all laughed. All but Maria, who, when she heard the story, later tried to drill her child correctly.

How dear and serious she was, Mariano told himself. If only he could spend more time with her and his little boy. Already he sensed that his time of relative leisure would soon be cut off.

Meanwhile, through all the windings and variations of the creoles' plots, the Commander General Santiago Liniers, who would be named temporary Viceroy in May, 1808, set a pattern of supercilious gaiety and indiscreet abandon. He rode through the streets in a coach with his arm flung around his mistress, La Perichona, who shocked provincial matrons in her decollete dress. The next day he might join a religious procession as a penitent. On the whole he scandalized the old Spanish families, and at the same time entranced — for a while, at least — many adventurous young blades among the creoles.

All Liniers' lighthearted swaggering could not hide from the more serious patriots, however, that funds in the treasury were reaching a new low. Was not the colony undergoing expenses unheard of before? There had to be maintained the recently formed battalions of creoles — the Patricios — under the command of Colonel Saavedra, while other drains on revenue were the new arms factory and military commissaries and hospitals. In 1807 expenses had mounted so rapidly that new sources for public funds had to be found, and quickly.

Into this crisis of the budget Don Martín Alzaga, childishly vain Alcalde of the First Vote, began to step with his heavy and clumsy tread. Alzaga, wealthy Spanish merchant that he was, saw the budget crack-up as a means for his own advancement. Why shouldn't he be Viceroy, instead of this Liniers? Besides, wasn't Spain falling to pieces? Napoleon was demanding more than a subsidy now. A tricky fellow, that Napoleon, that "Pepe Botellas," who drank water instead of wine. Doubtless the Frenchman Liniers would hug up to him, even more than it was rumored he already had. Alzaga hatched plots with the Spanish Governor, Elío, of Montevideo, to throw Liniers out. In Montevideo an independent junta was set up, in defiance of Liniers. But in Buenos Aires the plan, which Moreno was asked to join, fell through.[1]

(Moreno's enemies, later, will make much of the fact that he had been named one of the Secretaries of this "Spanish" Junta. Yet no one knows whether he had accepted, and the evidence from his brother, Manuel, is that he had not.)

What was the background of Alzaga's revolt? The real roots were being sown across the ocean. In Spain, during the year 1808, Napoleon was giving the usual dictator treatment to neutral countries which stand in a dictator's way.

First of all, he had bribed the minister Godoy into offering no opposition to the advance of his troops. This so angered the Spanish people against their government that their king, Carlos IV, prepared for flight when a popular uprising at Aranjuez decided he should abdicate in favor of his son, Ferdinand VII. Meanwhile, Napoleon held Carlos IV and his queen captive. But the people were not fooled. Bonaparte's next step pushed them into open revolt.

This step was a forced declaration from the captive King Carlos that his abdication in favor of his son was null and void, and that instead of Ferdinand's rule, Spain should be put under the sway of the dictator's General Murat, who would be *"Lugar Teniente"* of the kingdom. Later, Joseph Bonaparte, Napoleon's brother, would take over the reins of government as king. This was the last straw. When Joseph entered Spain, he found the country already in open rebellion, with juntas of self government erected in Sevilla and Galicia, juntas which were supported by a new ally, England.

The news of all these different rulers came a little late to Buenos Aires. First, the Viceroy Liniers received a notice that he should order the colony to swear allegiance to Ferdinand VII.[2] This news came from the Junta of Sevilla, which was opposing Napoleon. General Castañas had won a victory against the French, and in Cádiz the French squadron and garrison had surrendered. But before the people in Buenos Aires could know of these events, Liniers received another notice to swear allegiance to Murat. Shortly afterwards a French emissary, the Count de Sassenay, whose ship had been pursued by British cruisers, arrived, breathless, in Montevideo. Here he announced that he was Napoleon's envoy and that he carried credentials from the Supreme Junta of Madrid, dated June 14.[3] His amazing message for the colony was that the latest ruler in Spain was Joseph Bonaparte.

When Sassenay came to Buenos Aires, the hostility in the faces of the people on the streets and the oaths against the French were so great that Liniers had to rush the Count off on a boat waiting in the harbor. Then it was that Liniers, himself, began to make mistakes.

Until now his chief opponents had been the Spanish monopolists of the Cabildo, headed by Alzaga. These Spaniards were against him not only because Alzaga wanted to be Viceroy, but for other reasons. Liniers' frivolity was probably only an excuse. The Spaniards' principal complaint was that, in order to fill the treasury, the Viceroy was opening the port to trade with Brazil and had greatly reduced duties on Brazilian products, as well as on exports from the Buenos Aires ranches. Liniers had done this partly in return for the liberal trade policy of the Portuguese monarchs, Carlota and Don Juan VI, who had fled to Río de Janeiro when their country was overrun by Napoleon. Naturally the Spaniards did not like this partial free trade, for it hurt their monopoly of smuggled goods which brought them such high prices. Soon, however, they will have found a more genuine reason for alarm in Liniers' conduct. It is this conduct that had been worrying Moreno ever since the *Reconquista*.

After the departure of Sassenay, Liniers made the mistake of issuing a strange proclamation. In it he postponed the oath to Ferdinand VII. He told the people that they "should await the fate of the mother country in order to know what authority would occupy the throne." He assured them of the appreciation they merited from his imperial and royal majesty, the great Napoleon, for their past triumphs. He exhorted them in Bonaparte's name to remain tranquil.[4] He even added that Napoleon would help them keep their high reputation by offering them "all kinds of aid"—presumably against the British, who had captured and burned Sassenay's boat.[5]

It was this proclamation which set off the fireworks. For by this time gazettes from Cádiz had arrived telling of the shameful way Napoleon had treated Spain, first demanding safe conduct through the country for his troops to take over Portugal. Then capturing the Spanish monarchs who, in terror, had abdicated in favor of their son, Ferdinand. And then imprisoning Ferdinand through a ruse, and turning the French troops against Spain, herself. To think that Liniers should promise Buenos Aires aid and praise from Napoleon, against whom the people of Spain had just risen in the name of their new and captive king, Ferdinand VII!

Oaths against the French grew louder and more menacing. From the Plaza, from the streets. In private meetings, young creoles thought up desperate measures.

One of these groups of wealthy young creoles had been holding secret sessions in Vieytes' soap factory for some time. This group, the *Club of the Seven*, was headed by Manuel Belgrano, who had been upholding free trade in the Consulate for years without success. Among the other members were Martín de Pueyrredón, the lawyers Juan José Passo and Juan José Castelli, and Nicolas Rodríguez Peña. It was Belgrano's plan to set up an independent monarchy in Buenos Aires and invite Carlota of Brazil to be regent. Yet Carlota's morals were even worse than those of the former Spanish queen, Maria Louisa, with her lover, Godoy. Belgrano knew this, but he explained that the Infanta Carlota would only be a figurehead and that the creoles would be the real rulers.

What did Mariano think of this group? Certain it is that he went to a few of their meetings, and that he felt kindly toward Belgrano, whose ideas of free trade he admired and whose copy of Condorcet's translation of Adam Smith he might borrow later. But his opinion of Carlota differed from that of the others. "Make Carlota head of the Viceroyalty!" he exclaimed. "But how foolish, *amigos*, to give to a sick body a sick head!" [6]

As so often with Moreno's remarks, this one, widely quoted, settled the matter, at least temporarily. In his mind not only Carlota, but the Viceroyalty, was sick. The system, he told himself, would need several prescriptions of tonic before it could be transformed into something better. He knew that one of the tonics must be a boost for the power of the Cabildo, which, with its provision for open meetings, was the only organ through which the people could express themselves. In fact, during these years he was taking several cases upholding the Cabildos against encroachment of their rights. A short while back he had taken a case for the Cabildo of the town of Jujuy against insults of the curates of that city. In this case he had said, "The magistrate augments the honor and brilliance of his magistracy in proportion to the increase of the dignity and distinction of the people. . . ." [7] As we shall see, in all these cases he is concerned with the people's freedom to express themselves.

Another such case was one for the Cabildo of Corrientes. Here he defended the right of the Cabildo to protest the seating in office of a man for alcalde who had not received the majority of the Cabildo votes. Later on, in 1809, he will take a case for the Cabildo of Córdoba against the Governor Concha's refusal to confirm the position of its duly elected members. Concha, by the way, was a Spaniard who had fought under Liniers and to whom Liniers had thrown the plum of the Córdoban governorship. Thus Moreno was trying to solidify the position of the Town

Council and to fortify in people's minds the maxim that not favorities, nor official whims, but majority vote should be the rule of government.

Moreno pointed out that it was by whim that the temporary Viceroy Liniers was now ruling. His preening and fawning in the reflected glory of someone else, particularly when that someone was a tricky, ruthless conqueror, was a quality that Mariano could not tolerate. Like his father, he, too, felt a tendency to lean over backwards at times to avoid ingratiating himself with someone higher up. When he saw an exaggeration of the opposite tendency in Liniers towards Napoleon, and would see it later in his future enemy, Saavedra, towards Liniers and all the Viceregal trappings, he could not countenance what he saw.

Luckily the people of Buenos Aires forced Liniers to go ahead with the oath to Ferdinand VII. It was not so much that they were in favor of Ferdinand, as that they were against Napoleon and in sympathy with the Spanish juntas which had sprung up to fight him. Mariano, himself, has left us a picture of the celebration of this oath in his articles called *Las Miras del Congreso*, of the year 1810. Here he attempts to show the people that they are bound by no obligation to a captive king which would keep them from setting up their own government. He says:

> Can a sensible man ever persuade himself that the coronation of a prince in the terms in which it was published in America could produce in the peoples a social obligation? A decree of the government brings into the public plazas all the employees and principal citizens; the first, as the agents of the new Señor who is to continue them in their jobs, the second, through the incentive of curiosity or the fear of the fine with which their absence would be punished. The crowd comes agitated by the same spirit which leads them to any noisy celebration. The Royal Alferez goes up to a plat-

form, swears there to the new monarch, and the boys cry *"Viva el Rey!,"* fixing all their attention on the coins the officials throw to them to make them cry louder. I witnessed the oath to Ferdinand VII, and in the atrium of Santo Domingo (church) the bastions of the adjutants were necessary to excite the enthusiasm of the boys which the money, itself, did not excite. Will this be an act capable of binding people with eternal chains?

Such a passage does not sound as if Mariano waited until May, 1810, to think seriously of independence. He was thinking of it on this day of August 21, 1808, (the day of the oath to Ferdinand) which he so graphically describes. And he must have been thinking of it again, on January 1, 1809, when he and his brother, Manuel, and Juan Larrea were drawn by the ringing of the Cabildo bell to the *Plaza Mayor* (now called *Plaza de La Victoria,* to commemorate the repulse of the second English invasion.)

Because it was on New Year's Day every year that the Cabildo held elections — that it went through the formality of renewing its membership — Alzaga had chosen this January 1 to ask Liniers to give up his position. When the bell rang, the Cabildo had just sent a delegation to demand the Viceroy's resignation, and there had been a delay. The *Cabildantes* wanted more support, and were ringing the bell to bring in other people on their side. There were two men in particular whom they wanted, men who had recently arrived in Buenos Aires: the Brigadier Joaquín de Molina, a representative of the *Junta de Sevilla,* and Don Ruíz Huidobro, an agent from the *Junta de Galicia.*[9] They also wanted Mariano and Julian Leiva, the two relators of the *Audiencia,* who would give their movement an air of legality. As they knew, Alzaga had asked these men, before, to be secretaries of the Junta he would set up.

It was not until Mariano entered the Plaza that he was asked to join the meeting. A glance at the agitated crowd convinced him that something should be done.

Spanish regiments of Galicians, Catalans, and Biscayans, in their reds and golds, lined the Plaza. Mariano noticed that there were no blue and white uniformed Patricios anywhere. But he had a good idea that they might be on the shore side of the fortress, where Liniers could easily call them to enter the fort through the sallyport. And he had heard that the Arribeños, creole soldiers from the hill provinces, were stationed in a garrison on the north of the Plaza, opposite the Convent of the Catiline nuns. He knew that if Alzaga persisted in including only Spaniards in his plans, if he refused to bring any more creoles into his government, there would be civil war. The Spanish regiments of the Plaza would clash with the creole regiments and all hope for real independence would die.

The syndic from the Cabildo was asking Mariano to come up to the meeting. Should he go? Could be prevent a premature clash?

The crowds in the Plaza were shouting, "We want Junta! Down with the Frenchman Liniers![10] *Viva el Cabildo y muera el mal gobierno!*"

His brother Manuel was urging him to see what he could do. He could no longer hesitate. He rushed up into the meeting. He was amazed at what he saw: a small group of Spaniards, headed by Alzaga, at whose side Dr. Julian Leiva stood at obsequious attention, rubbing together the palms of his hands, anxious to please and still more anxious to be rewarded by the Spaniards' favor. Leiva, his colleague relator at the *Audiencia*. Not one representative of a creole regiment was there.

Was Alzaga completely mad? He knew he must speak to him at once.

"Señor Alcalde!" he cried.

No sooner had he uttered the words than he was interrupted by the Bishop Lué, who drew Alzaga aside.

"This Moreno will take the reins out of your hands if you heed him, Don Martín!" he cautioned.

He should have known, Mariano thought. Ever since his winning for the Canon Fernandez in the case against him, Lué had resented his very presence. What of it? There was no time to lose.

"Señores," he cried, "without the adhesion of the creole regiments you are lost! They have been alerted. Are we to start a civil war? Who is our enemy? Only the man who would deliver us to Napoleon. Let us join with the creoles. Invite them to this council, Don Martín. I can have nothing to do with a government which does not represent the men of the country!" [11]

The two recently arrived Spaniards, Molina and Huidobro, turned to the Bishop to ask who this dark-eyed, dynamic fellow might be.

"One of the counsellors of the Court," Lué explained. "A scheming creole! One does best to ignore him."

Don Martín was holding out his arms for quiet. "Have you not heard the cries in the Plaza of 'down with the Frenchman?' Listen! There they go again!" His eyebrows arched, his large hands clasped the edge of the council table.

"For you, Don Martín!" Lué exclaimed. "They want you!"

The shadow of a vain smile traveled over Alzaga's features. "Let us go in a body to demand the Viceroy's resignation! Come. I, myself, will lead the way!"

Mariano has left them now. He descends the steps into the Plaza two at a time and is again by the side of Manuel. "They think only of their own importance," he groans. "They are blind. Blind!"

Alzaga and his henchmen are on their way to the fortress. Once inside, they demand, with little formality, that

Liniers resign his post. Are not might—and right—on their side?

But not for long. Scarcely before they can be answered Colonel Saavedra enters the palace room: Saavedra, accompanied by an impressive number of creole officers. Shocked and dismayed, Alzaga feels the blood drain from his face.

"We shall see who it is that the people want," Saavedra says. "Let his Excellency step out onto the balcony."

While his guards surround the Spaniards, Colonel Saavedra marches Liniers out the tall door to stand against the iron railing of the slender window balcony which juts towards the Plaza.

The effect on the crowd of this sudden move is electric. All at once the same men who, a moment before, had demanded, "Junta like in Spain!" began crying out shamelessly, "Long live Liniers!"

No doubt they are swayed by the presence of the creole soldiers, now entering the Plaza in large numbers. The Viceroy waves his hand gaily in response to their cheers. The debonair Liniers. Is he not after all their hero, especially when he is accompanied by the commander of the patriot regiments!

The next day Alzaga and the other conspirators of January 1 — held prisoners since the night before — are quickly sent into exile.

With such a futile ending Mariano might easily have become discouraged over any attempts at independence for Buenos Aires. Would not such efforts always be headed by self-seeking men? Why not take the path of least resistance?

Let the ideal die? That he could not do. The time was growing nearer, he guessed and hoped, when another opportunity would present itself. How soon would it be? How long?

VII

Moreno Defends Free Trade— La Representación de los Hacendados— *Hints of Independence*

"It is sad that the general good of a province needs a lawyer for its defense, even when the highest official is generously inclined to its development...."

... *"Why, Señor, what thing more ridiculous can be imagined than the sight of a merchant defending in a loud voice the observance of laws prohibiting foreign trade, and doing this at the very door of his shop, inside of which one finds nothing but English goods of clandestine introduction?"*

... *"There are some truths so evident that one insults reason with the pretense of demonstrating them. Such a truth is the proposition that free importation of goods which a country does not produce must help it as much as exportation of products which abound to the point of being lost for lack of exodus."*

... *"These lands annually produce a million hides, not counting the other skins, grains, and wax...so valuable to the foreign merchant;" yet "all our warehouses are full, for there is no chance*

*for an active exportation, and this has resulted in a
huge surplus which, occupying the capital of our
merchants, makes it impossible for them either to
make new purchases or to get a good price for the
hacendado. . . . "*

. . . *"Yet the freedom of American commerce has
not been prohibited as an. . . evil, but has been
ordered as a sacrifice by the colonies for the benefit
of the mother country. "*

. . . *"Yes, Señor, justice demands today that we
enjoy a trade equal to that of the other towns of the
Spanish monarchy. "*

. . . *"Reason and the famous Adam
Smith. . . who is undeniably the apostle of political
economy, show that governments in laws directed to
the general good, should limit themselves to the
removal of obstacles: that is the chief axis on
which. . . Jovellanos founded the luminous edifice of
his economic treatise on the* Agrarian Law, *and the
principles of these great men will never be proved
false. "*

. . . *"It was not the excess of riches. . . but
rather the excess of oppression which made the
English colonies revolt. . . . "*

*—Moreno, Mariano, La Representación de los
Hacendados, in Escritos Politicos y Económicos de
Mariano Moreno*, edited by Norberto Piñero, pp.
115, 119, 126, 132, 134–5, 164.

The above words were written by Moreno when he was
thirty years old. Upon reading them, one realizes that it is
no wonder that the enraged Spanish merchants, shortly
after he won "free trade," began to set up a movement to
send him into exile.

Moreno's free trade was a different concept from that

of the movement which, in the 1960s, gained ground both in the Atlantic Community and among the countries of Central America — elimination of tariffs and other barriers to the free exchange of goods between nations, a policy which has brought about as much greater prosperity to the regions which still practice it as Moreno's free trade would bring about for his *patria*, and more.

Though Moreno, if he were living today, would have counted himself a free trader in the modern concept — and so reveals himself as ahead of his time — in 1809 he was arguing against mercantilism, still carried on by Spain in its most rigid form. He was arguing against the practice of allowing the colonies to import *only* Spanish goods and to export *only* to Spain. Although this policy had been denounced by liberal Spanish economists such as Jovellanos and Campomanes, before Moreno no colonist had ever dared raise his voice with such boldness against it. No one had ever dared excite the sure revenge from the monopolists which such a stand would call forth.

What was it that prompted Mariano Moreno to take the obvious risk of incurring such opposition? Do we have here another instance of the pressure of environment and the inner make-up of a man joining forces to produce a landmark in the progress of society?

Through the work which made him famous in his time, even in Great Britain (where the *Representación* was translated into English) Moreno's character is seen to unfold with greater and greater clarity. (We must remember that in Moreno there was neither the cultured exhibitionism of, for instance, a Roosevelt or a Bolívar, nor the complete assurance, born of membership in a privileged class, so visible in Winston Churchill.) One senses that up until now he had been struggling with that side of his nature which had made him keep secret his plan to study law: the tendency not to disturb, too quickly, the smooth surface of his conservative background. As a youth he had been forced to grapple so strongly with the desire not to upset a relatively calm, studious existence that the outcome, when he did overcome this sensitivity and did exhibit the truth, was electric. It was like the quick flinging out of a wire from a too tightly wound wheel. As if he were telling himself, "If it is worth while at all to risk upsetting a precedent, then the result must be dynamic and productive enough to justify the greater effort I must make." It was for these reasons that Moreno could never interest himself in any group which did not think through to the most effective methods for independence.

Besides, there were few men among the active patriots of those early days who attracted him.[1] True, Castelli, Monteagudo, and Vicente López had all gone to the same university that Mariano had attended in Chuquisaca. López and Monteagudo, who were younger, probably went later, although Castelli may have been there at the same time. And we have reason to believe that Moreno knew Castelli fairly well, since it is with Castelli that he will go to the first meeting of the revolutionary Junta of 1810. But until a very serious joint enterprise would bring these men closer together, it is probable that many of Castelli's traits were the kind that would hold Mariano off.

He himself said of Castelli that he was "alinearado" [2] — like Liniers—in his impulsiveness and lightness. And surely many of the *Club of the Seven* were touched by this quality. Saturnino Rodríquez Peña, for instance, loved the dramatic and was always carrying off some escapade, helping the British General Beresford to escape his imprisonment, and plotting at Carlota's court for aid from the Portuguese. And as far as back as 1796 the brave future General Las Heras, who may have been at some of the meetings of the *Seven*, had taken part in the uprising of the students of San Carlos against their teachers. Another member of the *Seven*, Feliciano Chiclana, was to head a group of masked men in later days, assaulting and frightening one of the haughtiest judges of the Court, Antonio Caspe.

Thus the patriots of the *Club of the Seven* were quite different in temperament from the relatively studious and puritan Moreno. To be sure, they were not quite the type whom López describes as *forming* caudillos later among the gauchos. They were not the young men of honorable family who, either "through idleness or mischief, both natural conditions in a country without industry or political life, sought an outlet for their energy in the perverse instincts of a semibarbarian life" on the pampa.[3] But some of them approached this type. And, as such, their antics must have seemed like the pranks of overgrown adolescents to the more serious Mariano.

Moreno, then, held himself apart from them at first. Of the two men he might have known in Chuquisaca, Castelli was too impulsive and Monteagudo too much of a libertine to attract his intimate friendship. Yet from the time of the near overturn of Liniers on January 1, when the creoles realized that they, alone, held the key to the Viceroy's power (since it was their regiments which had saved him) a new spirit of self confidence and daring began making itself felt.[4]

Moreno could no longer brush aside the meetings of the *Club of the Seven* as play acting and melodrama of sword and cape. Besides, the news in the gazettes from Spain was every day growing worse. For instance, General Castañas' victory in Bailen had been nullified because of local rivalries between the *Junta of Sevilla* and the *Junta Central of Aranjuez*. The former had even prohibited Castañas for six weeks from marching on the capital after the surrender of

Dupont and thus the chance to knock out the French had been lost.[5]

When this news became known in Buenos Aires and Montevideo, rumors began to fly about how the Portuguese monarchs in Brazil would take advantage of Spain's fall to extend their rule over the Viceroyalty. Already in the interior, in Chuquisaca and La Paz, young hotheads, some of them led by Moreno's old friend, Medina, were setting up independent Juntas. But the lives of both these juntas were short. The one in La Paz was crushed early and the priest Medina sent to the dungeon prison of Lima—the dreaded *Las Casas Matas*.[6]

It was the news of his friend's sad fate as well as the notice of the appointment of a new Viceroy for Buenos Aires, whose sympathies he might enlist, that quickened Mariano's determination to do something for the creole *hacendados* if they should ask him.

The new Viceroy was being sent to Buenos Aires as a result of Liniers' troubles with a defiant Governor Elío in Montevideo. Cisneros, it appears, was a Spanish naval captain who had commanded a ship at Trafalgar and who did not relish his new post as Viceroy. When he arrived in Montevideo and heard of the revolts in Chuquisaca and La Paz he thought they were both movements against Liniers.[7] It was not strange, then, that he should feel his position of Viceroy as precarious. He felt this even more when Liniers, forced by the creole troops of Buenos Aires, went over to Montevideo where Cisneros had landed to tell him that the creoles would not submit to his rule unless he changed the man whom Spain had ordered him to appoint as Inspector General of the Buenos Aires regiments. Somehow word had reached the soldiers that Elío, Alzaga's partner, was to be put over them.

The *Club of the Seven* demanded at once that Cisneros

name another inspector. The new Viceroy complied. But the man he named, a Marshal Nieto who had come in his retinue, was, according to Pueyrredón who had met the Marshal in Spain, just as bad. Nieto was cruel, vain, and stupid.

It was thus an unpromising and cold outlook that greeted Cisneros on his final arrival in Buenos Aires, the night of July 30.[8] His instructions from Spain were to order Liniers to return to Europe immediately. He was also going to have to issue a pardon for the January 1 conspirators, the Spaniards led by Alzaga, allowing them to come back from Montevideo to Buenos Aires. The latter would be difficult because of the creoles' opposition. He was worrying about this difficulty when Liniers pleaded with him against the order to return him to Spain. Cisneros gave in temporarily and permitted Liniers to go to Córdoba so as to be near his friend, Governor Gutierrez de La Concha, the man against whom Mariano had taken the case for the Córdoban Cabildo.

Then Cisneros, who had alienated the Spaniards with his leniency toward Liniers, made a second mistake. He ordered the Patricios regiment of creoles to go to Chuquisaca and throw out the independent Junta. Since this Junta had been set up by popular election, just as the one in Montevideo under Elío had been erected, no one could understand why the first should be dissolved while the second was approved. There could be one reason only. Montevideo's Junta was composed of Spaniards, while Chuquisaca's contained creoles. The creoles in Buenos Aires, who had felt more confidence in the Viceroy when he granted their request not to put their troops under Elío, began to fall away from him.

Meanwhile, Mariano, in his position as *relator* of the Court, had a good chance to study this Viceroy who so desperately needed something to make him popular and, still more, to make him secure. Cisneros had decided that he must find extra money to maintain a strong army. Where would he get it? Liniers had met the financial crisis by relaxing trade restrictions with Brazil, and Cisneros himself had come with instructions from the *Junta of Sevilla* to open the port of Buenos Aires to trade with Britain in accordance with treaties of January 14 and March 21. After all, the British were giving aid to the Spanish juntas against Napoleon.

While Cisneros, timid and cautious, hesitated to carry out the order, Mariano saw his chance. He pointed out to him that the treasury would certainly increase its funds if the people as a whole could gain some profits and the government some extra revenue. Hadn't he, only the other day, Moreno reminded him, decided to stop the enforcement of the Patriotic Contribution because of opposition from Cabildos of the interior? [9] What would take the place of this income if not the low customs duties from an increased trade? Moreover, two British merchants were waiting with their ships in the harbor and asking to be allowed to sell their goods.

Mariano reminded the Viceroy of the petition of these merchants dated August 16, 1809.[10] Still, Cisneros hesitated. He sent the petition to the Consulate or Merchants' Guild and to the Cabildo for study. There were heated debates. Finally both bodies, after hearing Belgrano's arguments on September 4, decided to grant the request, but with so many restrictions that their assent was practically worthless.

It was then that the *hacendados* (rancher-farmers) and the laborers from both sides of the river came to Moreno. Would he represent them? [11] Would he *really* represent them?

They knew that he had drawn up a pardon for Alzaga and the other Spaniards of the January 1 conspiracy, and that for this reason he had been the object of criticism from some of the creoles. But they knew, too, that he had written the pardon under orders of the Viceroy. If Cisneros had been compelled to rely on this young creole lawyer for such a ticklish document as the pardon, then why should His Excellency not feel fortified, even forced, to grant free trade if the case for such trade were prepared by this same lawyer? Besides, Moreno had won risky cases before. He was daring. He was their only hope.

Moreno finished the *Representación* shortly before September 30, at which time it was presented. The people who heard his ringing words sat listening with mouths open — amazed, astounded. His argument was unanswerable, even when delivered by someone else as ordered by the embarrassed Viceroy. Moreno's wit, his sarcasm, his logic could not be mistaken. The words were his. Free trade at last and — who knows — other freedoms too. Let the Spaniards try to refuse them now. Impossible.

But wait. The Viceroy will not decide yet. He orders the *Representación* to be read again on November 6 before a junta of "watchful magistrates, intelligent leaders and citizens of recommeded honesty" [12] as part of a general paper, in which the legal opinions of Dr. Leiva and the *fiscal* Villota will also be presented. No, the wily trick—if it were a trick — would not work. Free trade was won and Cisneros knew it. Even though partially modified by Leiva and Villota the arguments of Moreno could not be pushed aside.

Cisneros opens the port to such an extent that in three-and-a-half months as much as 400,000 pesos swell the coffers of the customs house—a greater amount, by far, than had ever been produced in so short a time before. [13] But it is the *hacendados* who are benefiting the most. They are jubilant. A chance to sell and buy freely at last. They can hardly believe it.

Some of them are asking for copies of Moreno's argument, which, indeed, he had hoped to publish, as he explains within his paper. The "shortness of the time," he says, "has not allowed me to give all the extension to my ideas that I would like. If it pleases Your Excellency that I publish this paper, I will then add the reflections that I now suppress."

The Viceroy was not about to allow the publication. No wonder. Were there not hints in it for independence? But Cisneros could not suppress it. The *Representación* was translated into both Portuguese and English. With its distribution Moreno almost gains overnight the fame which Brother Cayetano had foreseen. The creole farmers and workmen—200,000 workers are mentioned in his brief— proclaim him their champion. At the same time his Spanish clients desert him completely. More than that. They urge the Viceroy to exile him to Spain. Cisneros would have liked to do so. Yet could he spare him? Buenos Aires was already so much better off financially. All the same, he offers Moreno a judgeship in the mother country—an undoubted honor. Moreno politely refuses.

Why was he considered so dangerous, at this point, by the Spaniards; and why so loved and sought out by the creoles? Without success, but still with sincerity, free trade had been upheld by Belgrano and even by Escalada before. It wasn't the arguments for free trade alone, then, nor just the prosperity it engendered that gained for Mariano at this time the epithet of "A voice that cries in the wilderness!" [14]

From now on he is also called the *hacendados'* lawyer. Phrases from the *Representación* begin to be quoted throughout the city. They are quoted everywhere the creoles meet. And these meeting places, ever since the days of the repulse of the British, had multiplied.

For the peons and poor gauchos and servant girls, rang-
ing from *Zambos* (offspring of Indian and negro) to *Pardos* (offspring of whites and mulattoes) to *mestizos* (half
Spaniard, half Indian) the favorite spots were the corner
grocery stores or *pulperías*. Here, for the least difference
of opinion, one man would challenge another to a duel.
There were not only physical duels with swords or knives,
but also mental duels of singing words and rhymes accompanied by the guitar. And here, even here, duels were sung
that used the dynamic words of Moreno's brief. Moreno on
one side, a Spanish smuggler on the other. This was what
the crowd loved. They immediately took sides, and pushed
their respective heroes out into the street in order to make
room for a dramatic and ostentatious fight with all the
flourishes, which they could watch and cheer from vantage
points on the tops of barrels and benches.

On a different intellectual plane the educated youths of
the city paralleled the peons' restlessness. They met to play
cards, drink maté or rum and discuss politics at all hours of
the day. The *Club of the Seven* had private meeting places of
its own: the house of Nicolas Rodríguez Peña, across from
the church of San Miguel on what is now Suipacha Street,
and the soap factory of Vieytes, probably on the other side
of the city where most of the warehouses were located, in
the district called Barracas, overlooking the river to the
south. Aside from these secret meeting places, there were
two very popular public ones: the Cafe of Mallco, across
from the College of San Carlos—the school had been converted into barracks for the Patriot regiment since the
British invasions—and the Cafe of *Los Catalanes*, near the
poplar-lined Alameda which followed the shoreline north of
the Fortress of the Viceroys.

Here men discussed the relative merits of the old

scholastic teaching rigorously upheld by Spain, and the new spirit of scientific inquiry and freedom of the individual preached by the French Encyclopedists, the North American political scientists and the liberal Spaniards, Jovellanos and Campomanes. They deplored Spain's closure of the *School of Navigation and Design*, founded at the urging of Belgrano to teach mathematics and science. They discussed also the free trade policies of Brazil, and speculated as to whether Carlota could be trusted as a regent for the colonies in case Spain's popular governments should fail. And they voiced their consternation and dismay that even since January first, when the Cabildo had been reorganized to a membership half European and half American, the body as a whole still sided with the Spanish monopolists. What barbarity! Then comes November 6 with the *Representación*. The words of Moreno throw all other speculations into the background. Hadn't Moreno even hinted at independence—a new nation? *Could* it happen?

There is special excitement at the *Cafe of Los Catalanes*, on Congallo Street, near the Alameda. Today, since the Viceroy's closing of Mallco's some time before, it is more crowded than ever. The *Club of the Seven* has just come through the door, preceded by its message boys, the young mail carrier, Domingo French, and the treasury clerk, Antonio Berutti. They pick their usual table and the waitress who knows them well brings at once two gourds of steaming maté. At some of the other tables men are playing cards, while another group gathers around a billiard table in the corner. The more conservative clients nudge each other, as other members of the secret club leave the various groups and come over to the table French and Berutti have chosen. They talk loudly about arranging a hunting expedition, then exchange messages and settle down to talk in a low voice about what really interests them.

They discuss Colonel Saavedra's possible antagonism toward Moreno, who has just won free trade. Of course Moreno's pardon for Alzaga, whom Saavedra's troops had captured that day of January first—that has irked the Colonel. But who knows, Moreno may bring forth the best cure for the sick body of the Viceroyalty after all. He may even have exacted as a condition for his drawing up the pardon a promise from the Viceroy that he be allowed to argue the case for free trade that he has just won. And you can't deny that four years ago he put the Bishop in his place in that case defending the Canon Fernandez.

"Strange type, Moreno," one of the group says. "Like us, yet not like us. Easy to talk to if you know him, but hardly seeing you if you don't. Probably thinking of some legal point or principle. That dynamic way he expresses himself. And all those quotations from the classics and the laws of the Indies and history."

"He used them in the *Representación—cierto*. Phrases for independence actually if you study them in depth. Listen to this: 'One cannot tolerate the insolence of the Syndic of the Cabildo when he scornfully discounts this plan' [for free trade] because, as he says, 'it is only the *plebe* who are interested in it. This is an insult for which the honest workingmen of this city should demand an accounting, if they did not know that the man didn't realize what he was saying.' Bold, eh?" [15]

"Go on, *hombre*. This is what we need to convince the *pueblo*. Every man on the street. Go on!"

"Not like Moreno to go too far too soon. Listen. Let me finish. Here's what he says: 'If the attribute, alone, of being rich must be the requisite to receive aid for matters the people themselves cannot adjust, then they ought at least to be in a position where they could elect intelligent leaders. . . .'

Us, eh? *Nosotros.* Beat that if you can!"

"Crying in the wilderness. A voice crying in the wilderness," one of the older men says. "*Mira!* The Viceroy continues to trick us. But let Moreno keep up his daring. We'll follow him, no?"

"*Como no!* Here's something else he says. You'll like this, Cerviño. You remember how the workmen pitched in to dig that fortification you directed around the fort. You know, before the *Ingleses* invaded again. Remember? Here's what Moreno's brief dares to call the workmen, the *plebe*: he calls them the *most useful part of society.*[16] *Perfecto*—eh?"

Cerviño says, "I'm not sure that sounds like an argument for free elections by the people. But who knows?"

"How do you happen to remember all those words anyway, *amigo*? Do you have a copy of the *Representación*? The Viceroy wouldn't let him publish it. How'd you get it?"

"Man, don't you go to Mass? Secret copies have been made. Printed on that old Jesuit printing press. The priests are reading them at Mass. *Que te parece? Te gusta?*"

Later on in this same cafe where most of the future leaders and active agents of the revolution to come in 1810 were meeting, other phrases caught the imagination. Men loved to quote the way Mariano had addressed the Viceroy in one place in his brief by saying: "The Sovereign did not confer on Your Excellency the high destiny of Viceroy . . . in order to watch over the fate of the merchants of Cádiz, but over our own!" [17]

Again: "Is it just that our products become vitiated and lost because the unfortunate towns of Spain cannot consume them? . . . . Humanity groans with the slavery of men whom nature has created equal to their masters. . . . There are truths so evident that one insults reason with the pretense of demonstrating them. Such a truth is the proposition that free importation of goods which a country does not produce must help it as much as exportation of products which abound to the point of being lost for lack of exodus." [18]

Better still: "Yes, Señor, justice demands today that we enjoy a trade equal to the other towns which form the Spanish monarchy." [19]

And finally, in ringing tones: "I sustain the cause of the *patria!*"

The *patria*, of which Moreno was speaking, is already, to the *Club of the Seven*, the embryo of an independent and democratic country.

His *Representación* grows in fame. And with it the name of Moreno begins to be, among the ranchers and others, a byword for freedom.

VIII

The Beginnings of Revolution

"Castelli, although a fiery orator, lacked the...prestige to lead; Belgrano had position and Paso had natural gifts, but neither possessed the ardent spirit that the intense hour needed." But once Moreno is called to "take a position in the revolution, he fills the vacuum, mixing with the multitude, not in its midst, but at its head. He was the spiritual leader of the revolution."

Levene, Ricardo, *La Revolución de Mayo y Mariano Moreno*, Vol. II, p. 52.

After the *Representación* Mariano constantly received invitations from the *hacendados*. On the flat pampas he could usually spot the ranch he was going to visit from far away. There would be a stream nearby, lined by eucalyptus and willow trees, planted by the owner himself. But the most conspicuous landmark would be a huge ombú, whose giant trunk and spreading branches stood out in bold outline against the sky. Shaded by the ombú, the ranch house was picturesque, low swung, built of sun-dried brick with a thatched roof and a patio. Usually of one story, it would be flanked by the larger *galpón*, or barn, which also served as living quarters for the gauchos, as well as store rooms for grain, hides, saddles and numerous other supplies. Sometimes a covered corridor connected the house with the *galpón,* or simply formed a running gallery down the length of the house on the river side.

It was in such corridors that Mariano would discuss with his clients politics and literature. Or sometimes if the *hacendado* were called away, he would sit there alone and read. We are told by Manuel that "in order to contemplate better the beauties of the fields he would take with him the *Studies of Nature* by Bernardin de St. Pierre, which he'd read under a tree, in sight of the river, or in the corridor of some humble house where he would spend the day." [1] Apparently the *hacendados* revered and loved him enough to say "my house is yours," and mean it. They also felt free to leave him to himself if he wished. As strong and sometimes poetic individualists, the ranchers responded to the high-strung character of his nature and appreciated his need for seclusion and solitude. And already many of them were guessing the nervous preparation within him of a still further effort for his people when the time might come.

Did they guess how soon?

Days of comparative relaxation in the country did not last long for Mariano. In May, only six months after the winning of free trade, news came to Buenos Aires that practically all Spain had fallen to the soldiers of Bonaparte. Only the port of Cádiz remained free.[2]. It was to Cádiz that the members of the Sevillan *Junta Suprema,* pursued in anger by a disgusted populace, had fled. But the Sevillans had soon been driven out by the local government of Cádiz, which helped to set up, in their stead, a "Council of Regency for Spain and the Indies." No one in Buenos Aires was sure who all the members of this Council were. The only thing obvious to the young creole patriots was that the Council could have no real authority, since it had neither been appointed nor voted on by the people. Yet another fact stood out to Mariano in particular. This was that Cádiz, home of the monopolistic *Casa de Contratación*, had always ruled against any liberal policies for Buenos Aires, and had even caused the Council to revoke, lately, a gesture for free trade.

What, Moreno asked himself, would the Viceroy, whose sour disposition was showing up more often these days, decide to do? He did what sounded like a plot to the creoles. He issued a proclamation to the city to remain quiet, while he consulted with the other Viceroys on how America should be ruled.

"Remain quiet, please, like good subjects!" This is the way the soldiers and the creole clubs interpreted the news. What an insult to their manhood, their intelligence, their rights!

After reading this proclamation, sergeants and corporals rode furiously throughout the city, alerting the members of the citizen militia to be ready for an emergency, urging them to come to headquarters daily for orders. As usual the *Club of the Seven* was taking an active part. On May 19 it held a meeting at Nicolas Rodríguez Peña's house. That night the commanders of the creole troops joined the club. All but the head of the Patricios, Colonel Saavedra, who had recently fallen out with Belgrano.

Tonight the young creoles are excited and inspired. They speak of the rumor that the Viceroy Cisneros may be calling Liniers and Concha from Córdoba with three thousand men to crush any possible creole revolt. They discuss the frightening possibility of a coalition of all the Spanish governors of the interior. Goyeneche of La Paz, Sanz of Potosí, and Nieto of Chuquisaca, who had led the expedition north against the creoles' early juntas there, all could be counted on to lead armies against any popular uprising. At the same time Montevideo's Spanish junta could use its ships to blockade the port—all this in case the creoles of Buenos Aires should wish to rule themselves.

"*Dios*, who has a better right to rule us now?" Belgrano asks. "In this case can we let anybody's threats stop us?"

On May 19 every creole knew, however, that nothing could be accomplished in the way of a popular government without the support of the Patricios under the command of Cornelio Saavedra. And Saavedra had remained away from the meeting. Only José Castelli knew that he was sulking it out in his *quinta* at San Isidro, just outside the city. Castelli offers to write a note to fetch him.[3]

On the next night, May 20, these young creoles, together with Colonel Saavedra, decide to ask the Viceroy to call a *Cabildo Abierto* to decide what government should be set up. Yet by the evening of May 21, the Viceroy has not made up his mind. He has only said that he would call the Cabildantes the next day to see what sort of program could be arranged.

That night creole soldiers guard not only the fort, but the houses of all the powerful Spaniards. The guards are a critical necessity. They must prevent any messengers leaving for the interior—for those towns still subject to royal Spanish governors with their trigger-ready troops.[4] When May 22 dawns the people fill the *Plaza de La Victoria* and call out with one voice a demand for *Cabildo Abierto*. Even friars ride about armed on horseback preaching independence. Meanwhile the *Club of the Seven* continues to meet.

At this time Mariano did not attend the meetings at Rodríguez Peña's house. His brother has written that whenever his friends spoke of substituting for the colonial system a government of the country, he always applauded the idea, but, at the same time, from his knowledge of history and of the effects of the past servitude of the people, he held back, fearing that liberty might be cut in the cradle by civil war and anarchy.[5] Yet he was torn. Was it now or never? What was he waiting for? The colony should have more time to prepare, he told himself. All the same, with the knowledge that the *Junta Central* of Seville had been accused of selling out to the French and had fled to the Island of Leon, Mariano launches another of his startling phrases.

To Manuel and his friends he exclaims, "Spain has become extinct!"

It is one of those expressions which sums up in a nutshell the views which have been in everyone's mind since the minister Godoy, shameless "Prince of the Peace" of Basilea, has started appeasing Napoleon. The words "Spain has become extinct" catch fire and spread through the Plaza and the streets.[6]

With this expression to fortify them, the lawyers Castelli, Belgrano and Paso sit on the edges of their seats at the Open Cabildo meeting of May 22. The haughty Bishop Lué is speaking.

"I'm amazed," he says in effect, "that men born in the colonies could imagine themselves possessed of the right to discuss matters which are the privilege, alone, of men born in Spain, because of the conquest and the many bulls of the Popes!"

On and on the Bishop expostulates. He is in his element. How well he has ordered the Council chamber, on the second floor of the Cabildo, prepared to suit him! Chairs have been borrowed from the Cathedral church, and a handsome red velvet runner produced to cover the table on the platform.[7] On it Lué has placed a huge, ivory cross. Why, this room is almost his Cathedral! He goes on to speak as if he owned the city. The creoles can stand it no longer. They call out and cry for Castelli to answer the Bishop.

Mariano is sitting near the back of the room. With both hope and anguish he listens ruefully to the debates that follow. If only these creoles could hold their own in argument, if only they would insist on a junta of men born in the colonies who should rule instead of the Viceroy! *Instead of*—not with. If they should succeed in this, then he would take over and help run their government. He would form them into men: into administrators, army chiefs, educators, and editors! Supposing they should ask him. A terrific task. Could he do it?

While the debate continues he remains withdrawn. He is studying one of the men who has just taken charge of the meeting to recognize speakers. This man is his former colleague at the Court, Dr. Julian Leiva, the other relator who now, since Mariano had fallen out of favor with the Viceroy, has become the chief counsellor. Crafty and oily, and far too anxious to stay on the side that seems the safe one—that is Leiva. As far as resources and troops are concerned, the safe side would be the Viceroy's today. For as everyone knows all the troops throughout the Viceroyalty, with the exception of Buenos Aires, are under Spanish officers.

It looks now as if the creoles are winning out in the debate. At least they have won in their request that a vote be taken on whether to set up a junta to *substitute* for the Viceroy. Clerks are passing papers for the vote to be written out in secret ballot. From all the expressions of opinion it seems a sure thing. Surely the creole formula for setting up a junta of citizens which would *not* include the Viceroy is the one that will win. But with Leiva counting the votes? As Mariano searches the man's face, Leiva's eyes avoid him. Then it is true. This man will lie about the votes.... Mariano feels sick as he foresees the betrayal that will come.

The voting has gone on until a late hour. It is damp and

cold. Several of the men have left. Still Mariano remains in his seat, hunched up from the cold, lost in thought. Vicente López passes him and asks, *"Que te pasa, Moreno?"* [8]

"I've voted with you," Moreno answers, "because of the insistence of Martin Rodríguez." (Rodríguez was commander of the creole regiment of Hussars.) "But I've my suspicions that the Cabildo will betray us. Now I tell you we *are* betrayed."

López tries to reassure him by speaking of how they can count on Levia to put an end to any plot that is being hatched.

"Leiva, Leiva!" Mariano cries. "Yes, just confide in that *comodin*. You'll see what he'll do. On one side or the other he'll wash his hands like Pilate!" [9]

On May 24, Mariano's doubts turned out to be prophetic. Notices were pasted up in the *Plaza de La Victoria* and circulated throughout the city, saying that the new junta voted on by the Open Cabildo was to be headed by the Viceroy Cisneros, and that only two of its members were to be creoles. Those two would be Saavedra and Castelli.

On hearing this news the young creoles began lighting bonfires at the intersections of the streets. Men, women and children helped them, bringing sticks and branches to stoke the fires, while others ran about pulling down the notices. Once the flames shot up they started burning the fraudulent decree. With shouts of defiance they threw in every notice they could find. As soon as the decrees were destroyed the young men raced to the barracks.

Anger and commotion in the barracks of *Los Patricios*. The soldiers were declaring that if their leader, Saavedra, remained in the Junta they would not follow him.

At Rodríguez Peña's house—drama. Castelli has just stumbled in. He almost cries out the news about how embarrassed he is that he has accepted a position in the Junta headed by the Viceroy.

"What can I do?" he asks.

They tell him that he must resign and persuade both Saavedra and the Viceroy to resign too. Doesn't Saavedra know already that his troops will not support him in such a junta? Doesn't everyone know that the majority voted May 22 for a junta *without* the Viceroy?

The *Club of the Seven* has been daring before, but never so daring or defiant as it becomes on this night of May 24. The atmosphere in the city has been electric all day. Berutti and French had been parading the streets, beating drums and calling out that there should be another Open Cabildo tomorrow that would elect a junta which would *truly* represent the people. Tonight the Club is debating who the members shall be. Belgrano lies exhausted on a couch in the room next to where the men have gathered. Finally he can stand the arguments no longer. He jumps up to join the others. The expression on his face is exalted.

He is dressed in his blue and white uniform. Placing his right hand on the cross of his sword he cries: "I swear to the *patria* and to my *compañeros* that if by three o'clock tomorrow the Viceroy has not resigned, on my faith as a gentleman I shall turn him out with my arms!" [10]

Applause. Deafening. "We're with you!"

But who should form the new junta? The young clerk, Berutti, takes pen and paper and writes down several names. These names have been suggested many times before, but never before have they been thought of in just this combination. At any rate the list contains the favorites. The minute Berutti reads it aloud everyone congratulates him.

"*Hombre*, it's inspired—this list!"

All night long men on horseback ride through the town

securing signatures of further approval for the new Junta. What are the inspired names for whom these patriots seek the acquiescence of the people? Who have they chosen to head their new government?

Saavedra is to be President. Belgrano, Castelli, the priest Manuel Alberti, Miguel de Ascuénaga, Juan Larrea and Domingo Matheu—these last two, liberal Spaniards— are to be Members. And the Secretaries—the Cabinet—are to be Juan José Paso and Mariano Moreno. Paso will be Secretary of *Hacienda* or Finance, and Moreno, Secretary of State or Government and of War.

The Club has, indeed, been daring. It has chosen the new Junta itself. More than that, it has not even asked the man who will carry most of the burden whether he will let his name be used. Mariano Moreno was not even there. How will he receive the news?

IX

Moreno Becomes Secretary of Government and of War in the Revolutionary Junta, 1810

". . .what is most surprising [is] the fact that his mind could come down to the practical, the indispensable at each moment, with a clarity and an expediency that the most expert statesman might have envied him."

López, Vicente Fidel, *Historia de la República Argentina*, Vol. 3, p. 184.

Mariano was visiting in the house of his friend, Ignacio Nuñez, when Manuel brought him the news that he had been nominated for Secretary. During the day he had gone to talk to the troops and try to reassure them that the creoles would win out. With difficulty he persuaded them to be patient and do nothing violent.[1] Now, tired and in need of relaxation, he had started talking to Nuñez in a philosophical vein, trying to unwind from the tensions of the day. All the while the streets were resounding with the music of military bands, followed by crowds of people, including farmers and ranchmen and even priests and friars. It was evident from the heightening of the noise that the *Club* had come to a decision about the new Junta.

At that moment Manuel burst in. Elated, he gave his brother the news. Mariano took it calmly. He thrust his arm through Manuel's and said, "This needs some thought. Let's go home and decide what to tell them."

Nuñez exclaimed, "Surely you won't refuse!"

Mariano took him by the arm, thanked him for his hospitality and said, "I haven't refused. But we must examine the list. I'll let you know, Nuñez."

In a second he was on his way out the door with Manuel.

At home he walks up and down, stopping now and then to emphasize some point. Not yet has he said whether he will accept the position offered him. Manuel urges him to decide.

"I know," he says, "I know the dangers a magistrate will have to overcome in order to direct matters in such exposed times. Look, Manuel. The present change shouldn't limit itself to supplanting public officials. We must destroy the abuses of the past. We must develop an activity until now unknown, cure the evils that afflict the state, excite and direct the public spirit, educate the people, destroy or restrain their enemies. We must give a new life to the provinces."

"But Mariano. . . ."

Continuing to think as he walks, Mariano goes on, "If the government shuns this work, if it follows in the tracks of its predecessors, allying itself with corruption and disorder, it will be a traitor to the just hopes of the people. Unworthy of the high destiny which has been delivered into its hands. It's necessary, then, to blaze a new trail. One will have to steer the government in the midst of obstacles that despotism and venality. . . have piled up for centuries!"

"But will you accept?" Manuel asks.

"One moment!" Mariano turns to him, a sad, enigmatic

smile on his face. "Listen, Manuel. After the new authority has escaped the attacks to which it will be exposed simply because of being new, it will have to suffer those of the passions, interests, and inconstancy of those same who now foment the reform. A just man who is at the front of the government will be the victim of ignorance and emulation. The rest which I have enjoyed until now in the midst of my family and my books will be interrupted."

"You'll do it, then?"

"*Muy bien*, Manuel. I know. None of this can embarrass me in any point if it's certain that the general will calls me to take part in the direction of the cause. I'll not refuse. If my person is necessary, I cannot deny to my country the sacrifice of my individual tranquility . . . my time, my fortune, and even my life!" [2]

Manuel embraces his brother. And then another friend who has been nominated by the Junta comes by. Together he and Mariano investigate the circular to see whether their nomination has been legitimate. They scrutinize the signatures signed on the petition to make sure, as far as they can, that they are in the handwriting of the people who signed. It is only then after Belgrano and Mariano are sure the signatures are genuine that they will publicly accept.

The next day the Plaza is filled with men and women wearing the blue and white colors of the Patriotic regiment. They wear ribbons of these colors in their hats and in the buttonholes of their lapels. It looks as if there's going to be opposition from the Cabildo for the new Junta. For a long time the nominees have been forced to remain in the house of Azcuénaga, on the northwest corner of the Plaza. The people grow restless. There are cries of "Where is the Junta?"

Leiva comes out on the Cabildo balcony. He explains to the crowds that the new Junta cannot take office until the people as a whole approve the list nominated by the creole troops, the *Club of the Seven*, and their followers.

"All right. Read it to us!" someone cries. "We'll approve it right here. . . . What are you waiting for?"

Leiva consents. He reads the paper which is handed to him by Martín Rodríguez. To the list of names for the Junta, who had been nominated to govern provisionally, until a Congress could be called, there is added a stipulation that a military force of five hundred men should be sent to the interior provinces so as to assure free elections there of delegates to the Congress, which would meet in Buenos Aires to set up a permanent government. As Leiva reads the list and this provision, the people shout their approval.

It must have looked to Dr. Leiva as if this were the end for him. Yet he and the Cabildo hold one more trick up their sleeves. This is a provision that the Cabildo should watch over the conduct of the new Junta and remove it, if necessary. When Leiva makes this statement, someone in the crowd—one of the brown-robed Franciscan friars—pushes forward and cries out, "If the Cabildo can remove the Junta it must be with justification of cause and knowledge of the people!" [3]

Leiva answers, "The most Excellent Cabildo would never proceed without cause!" [4]

The people know how little truth there is in that statement. But they say no more, except to demand that the new Junta be sworn in at once.

Moreno, walking in the procession of the Junta that is headed for the Cabildo, has the right to be proud of two things he had been able to do already that morning, just after Cisneros' resignation. First, he had obtained from the Viceroy a pardon for Medina and had sent this pardon to the Viceroy Abascal in Lima, making sure that it would reach there before Abascal learned that Cisneros was no longer in power. Second, he had obtained another pardon for his client, Vicente Capello, the man who had been thrown into prison because of his insistence on taking possession of some land he had paid for but which a Spanish official was using as his own.

His remembering these two friends at this time shows at once a difference between Moreno's view of his new position and the views of most of the other members of the Junta. Some are in a high strung and altogether impractical and excitable state. This is natural, as their elevation to govern in place of the Viceroy is something unheard of until now. Also, they are reflecting the nervousness and ebullience of the creoles gathered in the Plaza.

The cannons from the fortress discharge a salvo when the members of the Junta come out of Azcuénaga's house and head for the Cabildo to be sworn in. At this moment the creoles go wild. Men throw their hats into the air. Women embrace each other.

The scene in the council room is impressive. The members of the Junta, with Saavedra in the center, line up facing the great council table. Each man places a hand on the shoulder of the one next to him, as they kneel in unison to take their oaths. Members of the regiments, in their many different colored uniforms of blue and green and gold, stand against the walls. The audience waits breathlessly.

The oath is to be administrated by the bishop. Now. There he is, directing each member of the Junta to place his right hand upon the Bible as he takes his oath of office. When Colonel Saavedra's turn comes he adds a few hesitant words of his own. "Only forced by the people and the turn of events do I consent to take this office." [5] Then he utters some more words about deference to the Viceroy.

Several of the more ardent creoles look at each other in wonder. What does he mean—"forced by events?" Does it possibly mean that Saavedra may want to go back to the Viceregal system later?

After the Junta was sworn in, on that late afternoon, Mariano went with the other members to the fortress and immediately began work on a circular to the interior towns. In this circular he asked the towns to send delegates to the new Junta, and told them of the military expedition that would soon leave to help them elect these delegates. The expedition would insure free elections without interference from the Spaniards.

A source of trouble later, this circular. A witness to the pressure and the incertitude under which Moreno was working. He changed it in the next few weeks by writing letters to the Cabildos of the interior in which he told them that their delegates, instead of entering the Junta itself, would meet in a Congress to form a constitution for the country. However, that night of May 25 the Junta and independence were still so new that it was thought the towns might not accept the creole government unless their delegates were invited to enter it. The Junta, of course, had been formed to protect the rights of Ferdinand VII, and this "mask of Ferdinand" was another device the creoles were forced to invent, in the beginning, in order to induce reception of their government.

Later, as Mariano guesses, there will be repercussions. Not tonight. Not the night of May 25. Now there is singing and rejoicing in the streets. Young creoles wander in bands throughout the town, serenading their sweethearts with guitars. And skyrockets trace their brilliant colors across the dark, night sky.[6]

Buenos Aires, although not free of the "mask of Ferdinand," is free of the rule of the Viceroy at last.

Señora Maria Elena Williams Balcarce de Moreno. Granddaughter
of Colonel Mariano Moreno and of Mercedes Balcarce. Great
granddaughter of the famous Mariano Moreno and Marcos
Balcarce.

Colonel Don Mariano Moreno
Son of the famous Mariano Moreno and Maria Guadalupe Cuenca de Moreno.
(Born in Chuquisaca, in the present Republic of Bolivia, January, 1805, died in
Buenos Aires July 7, 1876. Portrait now in the home of his granddaughter.)

Mariano Moreno.
Portrait.

*Daguerreotype of Don Mariano
Moreno.* In the home of Sr. José
Maria Moreno.

Dr. José Maria Moreno
Argentine educator and
politician. Son of Don José
Moreno. Picture in the
home of Sr. José Maria
Moreno. Born in Buenos
Aires Sept. 17, 1835, died
in Buenos Aires March 22,
1882.

Señora Maria Guadalupe de
Moreno. Wife of Mariano Moreno

Two miniatures belonging to the great Don Mariano Moreno,
brought from Chuquisaca to Buenos Aires:
Maté bowl and stirring tube
Incense burner, now in the home of Sr. José Maria Moreno

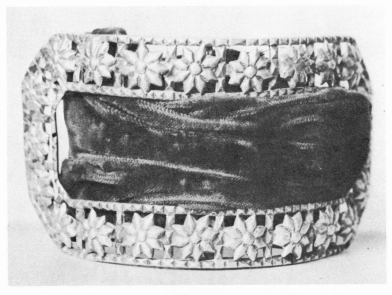

Shoe buckle belonging to Don Manuel Moreno, father of Mariano Moreno.
Now in the home of Sr. José Maria Moreno.

Seal of Don Mariano Moreno.
(Now in the home of Sr. José
Maria Moreno.)

Maté bowl:
Belonging to Don Manuel Moreno
(father of Mariano Moreno)
now in the home of Sr. José Maria
Moreno.

*Folding cup used by Don José
Maria Moreno* during the Paraguay
campaign.
(Now in the home of Sr. José Maria
Moreno.)

Monument to Mariano Moreno. In the Plaza Lorea, Buenos Aires.

Monument to Mariano Moreno. Scene of the inauguration of the monument and statue to Moreno in the Plaza Lorea, October, 1910.

Old Buenos Aires. Plaza de La Victoria. Market place and May Pyramid

Cabildo, Pyramid and Plaza de La Victoria in 1825, Buenos Aires.

Mariano Moreno, lawyer.
Secretary of First Governing Junta,
seated at his desk. (Reproduction of
the oil painting by P. Subercasseau)

Mariano Moreno—
Statesman, lawyer, author.
1777–1811.

Historic uniforms. (Of the soldiers of the Patrician regiment, 1810)

Homage to Moreno. Official carriage containing the memorial plaque on the occasion of the tribute to the memory of the great man upon the centenary of his death in March, 1911.

X

Repulse of Counterrevolution Freedom of the Press

"Without the brief lightning of Mariano Moreno's genius, the Junta would have been ship- wrecked in a sea of paper, would have been converted into one more expedient for the process of colonial agony. . . . In May, Moreno is transformed from a bored lawyer into a vehement journalist. . . . "

Ingenieros, José, *La Evolución de las Ideas Argentinas*, Vol. I, p. 189, p. 193.

The events of the next few months show an amazing activity on the part of Moreno. From May 26 until December 18, he was the life and soul of the Junta.

As we have seen, the Junta was provisional. (Its first proclamation would be issued in the name of the *Provisional Governing Junta of the Capital of the Río de La Plata to its Inhabitants and the Inhabitants of the Provinces under its Command.*) This transition period was going to be the most difficult. Although the Viceroy no longer ruled, he was still in Buenos Aires, and both he and the members of the Court were behaving strangely. They avoided mixing with other people, and when they did go out, they were more withdrawn than ever. Mariano knew that he must arrange for them to swear public allegiance to the Junta as soon as possible.

Until they do, the actions of the ex-Viceroy and the Court are evidence of the extreme danger surrounding the Junta. Moreno's first step now is to plan for the Junta to stage a celebration at which allegiance to the government would be sworn to by all the former Viceregal magistrates. Meanwhile, the new government was actually in a state of uneasy balance, sitting on one end of a see-saw where only firm and diplomatic guidance could prevent a collapse. It is more and more evident that to Mariano Moreno the task of supplying that guidance has fallen.

What, he asked himself, had Cisneros been doing since the resignation to which he had agreed on May 24? One of his activities was to write his friends to prepare for a counterrevolution. As early as May 19 his daring in this respect had been greatly encouraged by receipt of an offer of help from Liniers, the colorful French adventurer who had preceded him as Viceroy and who was still in Córdoba, not too far away.[1] Then on the night of May 25, when the creoles were celebrating their Junta with songs and serenades and brilliant fireworks, a young Spanish messenger named José Lavin stole out of the city with Cisneros' answer to Liniers. His answer was a quick authorization for the Frenchman to put himself at the head of an army of the interior which would help Cisneros overthrow the Junta.

No wonder Cisneros rested so smugly in the house of his friend where the Junta had allowed him to take up residence. He was playing an astute double game. Both he and the judges had signed the Junta's circular to the interior, requesting that delegates be sent to the new government. For temporary public consumption they had sanctioned the revolution. Meanwhile, Cisneros wrote to one of his friends:

> I shall try to leave the city, but if this is denied me I shall flee either to Montevideo or Córdoba, whence I shall exhort the other provinces to take all measures possible to restore order and put down the factious. . . . For if I have not left until now it is because I am watched incessantly.[2]

Without any proof as yet—for the ex-Viceroy's letters had not been intercepted so far—Moreno sensed the game which this man and the judges were playing. He knew he must challenge them, and soon.

He began by being extremely courteous and lenient. Four days after the revolution, he told Cisneros he "would enjoy all the honors, distinctions, and privileges which the laws concede to your military grade and to the viceroys who have been and remain in the district of their command." [3] Then Cisneros' house began to be the center of complaints against the Junta. On top of this, the ex-Viceroy and some of the judges refused to answer the Junta's note inviting them to be present at the official swearing in of the new government on May 30.

At once Moreno sent messages demanding a reply to his invitation. Through his insistence the judges and the ex-Viceroy did appear on May 30, together with the Cabildo and other organizations, to answer affirmatively the following request of the Junta:

> Do you swear to God our Señor, on these Holy Scriptures, to recognize the Provisional Governmental Junta of the Río de La Plata, in the name of Señor Don Ferdinand VII, for protection of his august rights; to obey its orders and decrees, and not to make attempts directly or indirectly against its authority, and to aid and respect it both publicly and privately? If this you do, may

God sustain you, and if not, God and the *Patria* demand
it of you and hold you accountable.

All will swear and all will die before breaking the
sacred obligation imposed.

The *Plaza de La Victoria* is filled with people on that
day of the oath to the new government. Among the crowds
there are a few British sailors with their officers, in their
Royal Navy blue uniforms. And there are creole as well as
Spanish merchants, and, of course, here and there, one of
Moreno's *hacendados* who has made a special trip in from
his hacienda. Some of the judges take the oath with reservations, saying the "Court" swears allegiance always within
the concept of the Junta's dependence on the government
that would be legitimately established in the Spanish peninsula.[5] Nevertheless, Cisneros and members of the Court,
Cabildo, and other organizations do swear their allegiance,
and the oath is followed by a *Te Deum* and a mass in the
Cathedral, and later by a *Besa Manos* in the fortress palace.

Why then, Moreno asked himself, have the judges
refused to answer his second note asking them to send a
notice to the provinces recommending union with the
Buenos Aires government? He sends another message
challenging the Court on this count. He writes:

Señores, answer freely and frankly, for the Junta
acts from now on responsible for any results. For, if in
the installation of this government there is discovered
any attempt against the sacred rights of our august
monarch, the ministers and vassals do not fulfill their
duty by closing themselves up in their houses and main-
taining a profound silence. Instead they should sustain
with energy the cause of the King, shedding for this
cause even the last drop of their blood, and showing the
people that fidelity, like religion, has its martyrs![6]

The judges squirmed when they received this challenge.

It looked as if that young upstart of a counsellor, who used to help write their opinions, meant business. But if they could only keep him guessing, until help from Liniers and Concha and the other royal governors arrived!

They answered Moreno's note with a sudden demand that the Junta swear allegiance to the Council of Regency in Spain. It seems that the judges had just received news through unofficial channels from Cádiz that this Council, set up January 29 to take the place of the discredited Junta of Seville, had published a decree which purported to be more lenient to the colonies. The Council was going to convoke a parliament to which the colonies would be allowed to send, for the first time in history, a delegate of their own. The only two ironies in this situation were: first, that there was to be just one delegate for each Viceroyalty; second, the Council itself was without real authority, since it had been established on the Island of Leon in virtue of a decree expedited without a date and signed only by its president, the Archbishop of Laodicea, without consent of the *cortes* and the nation. And now the judges and the ex-Viceroy, who had themselves hesitated to recognize the Council, demanded that the Junta swear to it and elect a delegate to its parliament.[7]

Moreno found little trouble in ridiculing this demand in his note of June 7 to the judges:

> Why should one expect of the Junta an act that was not thought the duty of the Señor Viceroy? Does waiting for those solemn acts, which according to the laws should decide the...legitimacy of the new government, run some risk? Do you...distrust this Junta or the people? [8]

On the same day that Moreno threw down this challenge, he started editing a newspaper called the *Gaceta*. He asked everyone to contribute articles to the paper and he himself wrote later the lead article on *Freedom of the Press*. It was through the *Gaceta* that he hoped to educate the people more fully in self-government and to explain to them all the Junta's actions.

The article which launched the *Gaceta* is also a famous one. In it he said:

> The populace has a right to know the conduct of its representatives.... The Junta could...rest on the gratitude with which its tasks are publicly received. But the provisional quality of its installation redoubles the need to assure, in all ways, the concept of the purity of its intentions.[9]

As we shall see, Moreno, alone, of all the members of the Junta, was to insist on and reiterate, as time progressed, the provisional position of the new government. He was much more concerned with the great task of creating the foundations of a democratic constitution for the future nation than he was with the power of a permanent rule. He went on to say:

> ...an exact notice of the procedures of the Junta, a continued public communication of the measures it agrees on to consolidate the great work which has begun, a sincere and frank manifestation of the obstacles which are finally opposed to its installation and of the measures it adopts to overcome them are its duty in the provisional government which it exercises....
>
> For the achievement of such desires, the Junta has resolved that a new weekly periodical should be issued, with the title of *Gaceta of Buenos Aires*.... In it will...be published the official discussions of the Junta with other chiefs and governments; the state of the *Royal Hacienda*, and economic measures for the people's betterment. And a frank communication of the motives influencing the Junta's principal measures will open the door to views which anyone who can contribute

with his knowledge to better accuracy of judgement might desire to give.[10]

This invitation for writers to point out to the government, in a free and public press, ways in which it could improve, was, of course, a complete novelty in the colonies.

It was on June 21 that Moreno wrote his editorial on *Freedom of the Press*, published two weeks after the *Gaceta* was launched.

While upholding freedom of expression he recognized the difficulty of carrying it out in a land where such principles had been denied for so long. He wrote:

> Let us be, for once, less partisans of our old opinions; let us have less self-love. Let access be given to truth and enlightenment; let not the innocent liberty of thought in matters of universal interest be repressed. . . . Truth and virtue have in themselves their incontestable defense; by force of discussing them and ventilating them they appear in all their splendor . . . ; if restrictions are opposed to discourse, spirit will vegetate like matter, and error, lies, prejudice . . . will be the device of nations, and will cause forever their oppression, ruin, and misery.[11]

Earlier in the article he had pointed out that the history of other lands showed the obstacles against which truth and freedom had been forced to struggle. He said:

> Socrates, Plato . . . Anaxoragas, Virgil, Galileo, Descartes, and other scholars who tried to effect . . . the felicity of their compatriots, initiating them in enlightenment and useful knowledge and uncovering their errors, were victims of the furor with which truth is persecuted.

And yet he argues:

> Let us know that man will be born in the most shameful brutification if he is not given an absolute freedom . . . to speak on any matter which does not oppose . . . the holy truths of our august religion and the determinations of the government.[12]

Moreno's freedom of the press, therefore, had its limitations. But it was still a far cry from the inquisitional methods of Spanish rule, and thus a long step forward in the emancipation of the people.

In such an atmosphere of emphasis on truth how could the judges' treason go unnoticed? Would Moreno be able to force their deceit into the open?

Unfortunately, while he was trying to create an atmosphere in which the old leaders could no longer play a double game, the younger, more hotblooded revolutionaries who had formed themselves into a new club, boldly called the *Club of the Factious*, were not so patient. They decided they could no longer stomach the two-faced attitude of the Court.

On the night of June 10, a Sunday, Feliciano Chiclana and a group of these boys met together to plan an escapade that would put the fear of God into the most hated of the judges—the criminal attorney, Judge Antonio Caspe. The young boys dressed themselves up in long capes and put on black masks. Then they sent a note to Caspe saying that President Saavedra wanted to see him.

The haughty judge, who wore knee breeches and a short cape and carried a gold-headed cane, went to the fortress that night to find that Saavedra had not sent for him after all. Then he started home.

As he crossed the drawbridge into the Plaza, he noticed troops of armed infantry at the four corners. All at once four masked men, in capes, were walking swiftly in his direction.

"Who are you?" one of them asked.[13]

"I am the fiscal of the King!"

One can imagine the laughter of the Factious, who had, in their minds, already discarded both the king and his officials.

Suddenly one of them shouted, "The 'fiscal of the king!' That's just who we want!"

The boys were enjoying themselves. They drew out their swords and flourished them. Caspe started running for his life.

"Kill him!" a voice cried.

The judge's knees began to wobble. The night was unusually dark. No moon, few street lamps. Out of breath from running, Caspe stopped to snatch a candle from the door bracket of a private house. The boys surrounded him. He beat at them with his cane, pulled himself loose, ran into a post, and fell headlong into the street—his legs sprawling, his arms rolled up in his cape.

The boys—convulsed with laughter—decided to call a halt. Quickly they lifted Caspe to his feet. Not knowing what else to do, they escorted him home.

At the door of his house no one answered their knocking. A little ashamed, they knocked again. Silence. They began to ask themselves what would happen if the Junta—if Moreno—should hear of their prank. They began to think of returning home themselves. But what to do with this old judge, who had sent so many innocent creoles to prison?

"Leave him to the Devil to take off!" one of them shouted.

The next instant they disappeared.

Moreno did hear of the incident, for Caspe reported it. The judge, however, did not name his attackers. He could not, for, in their masks, he did not know who they were.

The next day, June 11, Moreno issued a police ordinance for patrol of the streets. By this order, the alcaldes of each section of the city, accompanied by an armed force of selected, responsible citizens, were to make the rounds of their neighborhoods every night, "not allowing anyone to carry arms." The patrol was also to prevent gatherings at late hours, and was to punish anyone who, "by word or deed, sows division or discontent." [14]

Moreno's wording of this ordinance, published in the *Gaceta,* was outstanding for two reasons. It showed his serious conception of the people's responsibility in setting up their own government. It also showed his view of the elected officials' duty to those people. And it refuted later accusations from the Viceroy of Lima that the Junta's government was one of violence and bloodshed, that, in Buenos Aires, the "streets flowed with blood." The ordinance, on the contrary, demonstrated that Moreno stood for order and that he was neither Robesperian nor vengeful, as his enemies would claim later. In contrast, the substance of his decree was, quite clearly, an attempt to protect from violence his own worst enemies. This is what he said:

> Since you deposited the power in our hands, your own remain linked to obedience. Your oath confirmed obligations consequent to our installation. And the confidence owed to the free election of our persons ought to remove all spite, with public safety confided to the zeal and vigilance of those who govern. Ambition did not open the road to those who form this Junta. You voluntarily called us. And it has been no little sacrifice to receive upon our shoulders a weight, superior, perhaps, to our strength. We have consecrated ourselves to your welfare and we shall die to achieve it. But, also, you have subjected yourselves to our government and you should be obedient to our precepts.
>
> The Junta reminds you of those simple principles which you swore at the time of its installation, because last night they were scandalously violated. The Señor Criminal Attorney, on retiring to his house, was insulted in his person. And if his aggressors have not shown the vile interest of assassination, they have surely been agitated by vengeance, which in the mistakes of its origin...displeases this government.[15]

Then came the provision for the nightly patrol to prevent such acts of vengeance in the future.

While Moreno was writing this ordinance, and trying to effect a peaceful transition to a more democratic government, the judges and the ex-Viceroy's underground movement for counterrevolution was going forward. These men began dispatching orders to the Cabildos of the interior towns, telling them they must swear to the Council of Regency in Spain. The results of their action became known to the Junta in critical fashion.

The Cabildo of Buenos Aires had received news from the Cabildo of Córdoba that it would soon send a deputy to the new government and that it was disposed to recognize the Junta. But when the secret message from the judges arrived, on June 14, ordering the Córdobans to swear to the Council of Regency in Spain, the members of the Cabildo decided to revoke their recognition of the Buenos Aires Junta.[16]

Moreno, as Secretary of State, knew that the Junta could not hold its position if these countermands from the old *Audiencia* and the former Viceroy continued. They did continue, for Montevideo soon followed Córdoba's example. There was no doubt as to what he must do to meet the danger. Increasingly, it was to him that the Junta looked for direction, for it had been apparent from the first that Moreno had not entered the government in order to turn back later to the old way of life. He could never have said, for instance, as the President Saavedra had said in his oath, that the virtues of the Buenos Aires residents "which had proved themselves against a foreign sovereign had a greater obligation of correct attitude toward the magistrates of a Sovereign whose captivity everyone mourned, begging Heaven to return him to his natural throne." [17]

The last thing the Secretary of the Government wanted

was a retrogression into the old order. If the former magistrates were already attempting to undermine the Junta,
there was only one thing left for the government to do. That
was to send them into exile.

On June 22, Moreno called a meeting of the Junta to
make his proposal and put it to a vote. As soon as the motion
for exile was approved Moreno and the Junta called the ex-
Viceroy and all the judges, except the two eldest, to the fortress for a conference. They came in their best court dress,
carrying their gold-headed canes or *bastones*—evidence of
how difficult it was for them to believe it was the Junta
which was ruling. Once inside the fort, however, they
learned otherwise. Castelli and Matheu told them that their
continued residence in the city was dangerous, and that
they must embark immediately. In fact, there was a ship
waiting in the harbor to take them to the Canary Islands. In
a few minutes the Junta's guards were escorting the conspirators to the ship.[18]

History has given Moreno both credit and blame for
such acts of firmness. As Secretary of State and of War, his
decrees and letters—now part of the national archieves of
Argentina—were responsible for the bold defiance to all
moves of counterrevolution. Still, it is also a matter of
record, in the testimony of Belgrano, that decisions for all
measures, exile included, were always made by a majority
of the Junta.

From what we know of Moreno's character and
background, in comparison to that of the other members, it
becomes more and more evident that it was he who felt the
greatest responsibility for saving the government into
which he had been virtually thrust. Matheu and Larrea,
who were both peninsular Spaniards—not born in the colony—could never feel the creoles' efforts at self government as keenly. Azcuénaga, who was wealthy, could easily,

because of his financial power, secure a position under a return to Spanish rule. Belgrano and Castelli were brave and devoutly patriotic, but neither possessed the imagination or foresight necessary for handling the old magistrates which Moreno had learned from his practise with the Court. The same could be said of the priest Alberti. As for Paso, the Secretary of Finance, who was a learned lawyer, he, too, lacked Moreno's experience in working with organs of the former government such as the Cabildo and the Court. Finally, there was the President Saavedra, who would not have entered the Junta at all unless his soldiers had refused to support him otherwise. Unless, as he himself said in his oath, he had been "forced by events."

Moreno alone, then, was left to undertake a persuasive role for the others. No wonder that he had said in his ordinance for the neighborhood police patrol that it had been no small sacrifice to receive such a "weight upon our shoulders." For his having risen to this task in the crucial days of attempts at counterrevolution, not only Buenos Aires, but most of Spanish America, as we shall see, will owe her eventual independence.[19]

Meanwhile, his accomplishments have placed the Junta one rung higher on the ladder of security. He has started a *Gaceta* to educate the people. And as a result of his challenges, the Junta has discovered the treason of the former Viceroy and the judges and has sent them into exile. But Moreno's troubles were not to end here. In fact, they were just beginning.

XI

Consolidation of Democratic Rule Expedition to the Interior

> *"And all this varied and multiple labor [of Moreno's] was realized in the midst of the absorbing attentions and terrible cares of the war undertaken against the forces of the mandatories of Spain, who were already in possession of the greater part of the Viceroyalty!"*
>
> López, Vicente Fidel, *História de La República Argentina*, Vol. iii, p. 183.

Partly as a result of the judges' order to swear to the Council of Regency, but more probably because of a desire to keep a stranglehold on their districts, the Spanish authorities, not only of Córdoba and Montevideo, but also of Paraguay, defied the Junta's request to send deputies to Buenos Aires. By this time Moreno had corrected his first circular and asked the towns to send delegates not to enter the Junta, which was provisional, but to enter a Congress which would draw up a constitution for the land. And now the Junta is being notified from several regions that there will be resistance.

What will Moreno do in the face of this threat?

His first act was to try to bind the towns closest to

Buenos Aires to the Junta, and, at the same time, to prevent communication between Spaniards in Buenos Aires and Spaniards of the interior and Montevideo, situated on the eastern bank of the La Plata river. The Viceroyalties had been divided into Intendencies in 1782, each under a royal governor, and to these Intendent Governors had been handed many of the functions formerly exercised by the Cabildos. It was therefore logical and necessary for the Junta to set up its own appointees in the towns included in the Buenos Aires Intendency. Among these towns there were, in the order of their distance north from the capital, Santa Fe, Corrientes, and the settlements of Misiones. All were small villages in the section called Entre Ríos, between the Uruguay and Paraná rivers. To each principal town Moreno sent a military governor who would be directly dependent on the Junta and whose duty was to fortify these sections against the aggression threatened from Montevideo and Paraguay.[1]

To further secure the position of the Junta, he issued a decree on July 31, 1810, that no one could leave Buenos Aires, that no ship captain could conduct passengers without a license, and that all private firearms should be relinquished.[2] The decree also mentioned punishment for anybody distributing inflammatory papers against either Europeans or creoles, as well as for anyone corresponding with people in other towns in a way to promote discord and opposition to the government.

At the very least these measures were essential for the preservation of the Junta. Since the opposition promoted by the judges and the gathering of counterrevolutionary forces in Montevideo, Córdoba, and Paraguay, the government of Buenos Aires was virtually in a state of siege, quite as precarious, if not more so, than the young, independent

government of the North American colonies held together
by Washington's army.

While Moreno was still hopeful that he could win over
Córdoba and Montevideo by persuasive notes and by sending agents of the Junta to talk their governors around, he
began to realize that only an expeditionary force could talk
with a firm enough voice. True, the Junta was set up to protect the rights of the captive King Ferdinand (still imprisoned by Napoleon) and no one could say, officially, that
there was yet a revolt. In this respect the Junta's aim was
different, on the surface, from the English colonies' pronouncements, which were openly rebellious as well as based
on previous experience lacking in Spanish America. But
while the Junta could count the championship of Ferdinand
as an advantage, it was plagued by the disadvantage of being less well-equipped with an army and a military leader, so
far, than the North American colonies.

Thus the government had to press its subterfuge of
loyalty to Ferdinand to the hilt, and this Moreno did, clever-
ly and insistently, in his notes to the opposing towns. Meanwhile, racing against time, he tried desperately to band
together the pitifully small number of 500 men (called for in
the petition demanding the installation of the Junta.) These
men were to be sent as an auxiliary force to the interior
towns to protect the free election of deputies to Buenos
Aires.

The chief obstacle to the formation of this army, which
Moreno would increase to 1,300, was lack of funds. Washington had met the same discouraging lack of appropri-
ations for his troops from the Continental Congress.
Moreno was forced to appeal to the people themselves. He
made his appeal in the *Gaceta* for voluntary contributions,
starting them with a donation of six ounces of gold of his
own, which he could probably ill-afford.

Soon other contributions started pouring in. The humble of "both sexes" made donations, and even the slaves raised money among themselves and brought it in. There were some large donations, too. One man, Don Gervasio Posadas, gave 1,500 pesos, enough to pay the soldiers' salaries for six months. Belgrano, Larrea, and Matheu all donated the entire sum of 3,000 pesos which was the amount of their salaries as members of the Junta. Larrea, besides, underwrote a substantial loan subscribed to by business organizations. Saavedra, who in addition to being an independently rich man drew a salary of 8,000 pesos as President, contributed only 50 of these to the maintenance of the army.[3] Already the question mark occurs as to whether he was hoping secretly for a change that would make equipment of the army unnecessary.

Certain it is that in the days that followed, Moreno began to encounter a growing antagonism from the Colonel. Hardly surprising when the reservations of his oath on May 25 are remembered. It must have been a source of irritation to Don Cornelio, too, to know that while he was nominally President it was Moreno who was running the government. Indeed this irritation is reflected not only in his letters written later, but in the portraits where, dressed in his military uniform, Saavedra's thin, tightly-pressed lips are turned down and the carriage of his head is stiff and self-conscious. Although he was undoubtedly intelligent and his support of free trade in merchants' conferences had been courageous and sensible, both the portraits and his actions depict a man with little sense of humor. He is revealed as a person who would, in most matters, lean to the traditional rather than to the innovative side, and whose final decisions would be swayed more by a desire for the accepted formalities than by the "new" public spirit.

After the Junta had been safely installed and sworn to,

it is probable that Saavedra enjoyed his position. For one thing he had been granted the same "honors" as the Viceroy, in that he was given a special seat of prominence at all ceremonies and was driven about in the Viceregal coach, preceded and followed by an impressive escort of mounted guards, just as the former rulers had been. A royalist spectator of the day wrote: "The Señor Saavedra already goes with the escort of the Señor Viceroy. Many of them (the creoles) must be discontented because they did not receive any of the prize." [4]

In his educational articles on democracy in the *Gaceta* Moreno was, of course, treading a difficult, uphill course against the old habits of pomp and monarchy. For while the insignia of the previous rule were repugnant to the young revolutionary vanguard, still the people of Buenos Aires were not too eager to give them up. In general they believed they had erected a popular government to uphold the rights of the captive king. Too sudden a renunciation of the old formalities might have weakened support for the Junta. Moreno was wise in not objecting to the Viceregal honors in the beginning. Whether he would have been wiser never to have done so is another story.

Meanwhile his work to popularize the government was showing results. This work had to be carried out on so many levels that it is still a wonder that one man could have done it. On the educational level he decreed obligatory primary education, arranged for the publication of schoolbooks which would be distributed free to the children who could not pay for them, and raised teachers' salaries from 400 to 600 pesos a year.[5] He also founded a public library, the response to his request for gifts of books resulting in donations of four thousand volumes. As directors of this library he named Dr. Saturniño Segurola and his beloved teacher and counsellor, Brother Cayetano Rodríguez.[6] In these educational projects Moreno was joined by Belgrano, who had formerly worked zealously for better education with his school for *Navigation and Design* closed down by Spain in 1806.

Of the friendship between Moreno and Belgrano we have been given a brief glimpse. It is known, for instance, that "While Moreno subordinated the revolution to his genius, Belgrano...placed himself at his service. The one was the man of large political visions, of bold reforms, of initiative and revolutionary propaganda in every sense; the other was the man of administrative details, of patient labor.... Belgrano was the anvil of the Junta, Moreno was the hammer. Between them they forged the sword of the revolution. A common link united these two opposite natures: interest for instruction of the public." [7]

Unfortunately, with the looming of another counter-revolutionary threat, the "hammer" would soon be forced to lose its "anvil" to the army.

Meanwhile, Belgrano also helped with the military reforms which fell to Moreno's lot, as Secretary of War. Moreno saw that it would be fatal to send forth the military expedition unless he could set up some kind of permanent organization to train reserves and to drill an army to protect Buenos Aires. He planned to create this army from the levy he had ordered for all unoccupied men between 18 and 40. It was to Azcuénaga, who had also been placed in charge of the manufacture of arms, that he entrusted the management of these men.

As for the expeditionary force, it was to be made up of regiments from the old battalions formed to fight the British and from the lancers and dragoons recently organized by the former Viceroy for patrol duty. In order to improve leadership, Moreno established a cycle of conferences for officers to discuss strategy and organization. The conferences would take place in the homes of the colonels. At the same time he planned to open a School of Mathematics—a kind of West Point—for officers.

As usual with his innovations, the opening of this school was preceded by one of his articles in the *Gaceta*. While he spoke of the school, he also spoke of his plans for democratizing the army, where henceforth promotion would be based on merit instead of influence—a principle he would later extend to the selection of judges as well.[8]

Now while the expeditionary army to the interior was foremost in his mind, there were other immediate needs to attend to. Predominant was the need for the abolition of export taxes and the further reduction of customs duties. At the same time he must rehabilitate the ports of Maldonado, Río Negro, and Ensenada on the La Plata River, so that if Buenos Aires should be blockaded from the sea, supplies could be brought to these other ports and then inland to Buenos Aires. Most important of all, in the realm of diplomacy, he began corresponding with the British ambassador in Río de Janeiro, Lord Strangford, and winning him over to the Junta.

Indeed it was primarily because of Strangford's insistence that Moreno and the Junta were keeping the "mask of Ferdinand"—and with it the fiction that the chief reason for support of the Junta was prevention of the Viceroyalty's falling into Napoleon's hands. Because England was an ally of the unconquered part of Spain, Strangford had confided, he could not be friendly to the Junta unless it *did* continue to declare itself protector of the rights of the captive Spanish King. At the same time the British ambassador intimated that, in case the "mask" were kept, he would be very friendly, perhaps even to the point of lending aid.[9] Lord Strangford, of course, wanted the Buenos Aires port to remain open to British goods.

Moreno could easily remind him that this was much more likely under a government guided by the author of the *Representación of the Hacendados* than it was under a return to Viceregal rule.

With these accomplishments in the works Mariano again concerned himself with starting the military expedition on its way to the interior. The mission of this army was, as we have seen, protection of free elections for delegates to the Constitutional Congress to be held in Buenos Aires. Lately some of the gaucho scouts who were working for the Junta had caught royalist couriers—among them the son of Liniers—and found in their papers notes giving valuable information about counterrevolutionary plans in Córdoba. In one of these notes, the former royal official, Nieto, writing from Chuquisaca to the ex-governor Concha in Córdoba, praised the latter for having asked reinforcements from Río de Janerio, and for having sent agents to Montevideo requesting 500 mariners for Santa Fe.[10] Nieto went on to say that if Concha felt himself weak he should take no action, but should fold back towards Jujuy, where he, Nieto, would develop his "marvelous plan." This plan was as follows: If the insurgents should reach Jujuy first, he would destroy them in the pass of La Cueva, and in the naturally fortified position between Suipacha and Tupiza. His troops would march in time to punish Salta, would protect Jujuy and its faithful, subordinate Tucumán and Santiago del Estero, and,

> give Córdoba all the help it needs. With Santa Fe taken, Buenos Aires remains, with only its center and immense and useless pampas. And according to what I hear...it will be more or less of an effort for them [the Junta] to enter into their duties without forgetting the punishment we shall inflict on them.[11]

These plans of Nieto's were later to be supported by the

Viceroy Abascal of Lima who resolved on August 25 to aid Nieto with 2,000 men, to blockade Buenos Aires with the help of the Spanish warships in Montevideo, and to send troops and ships to Sacramento in order to start an attack on Buenos Aires and distract her from sending help to her expeditionary army.[12]

After the discovery of the plans, Moreno senses that the greatest danger is from the north and that Córdoba is its center. He decides to direct the expeditionary army, which by now had reached about 1,300 men, to leave for Córdoba on July 14. Later he would disclose in the *Gaceta* the threats of both Nieto and Abascal. Meanwhile some of these threats could be discounted, since Salta, Jujuy, Santiago del Estero and Tucumán had already pledged, in answer to Moreno's notes, allegiance to the Junta. It is these towns which will later swell the small army from Buenos Aires with contingents of their own.[13]

Thanks to the patriotic contributions of money it was a fairly well equipped group of soldiers that left from the bridge of Marquéz, located on the river of Lujon, about ten leagues west of Buenos Aires, on July 14. The place of departure was the field where the men had been drilling for the last month. Although they possessed fairly good guns and ammunition, the Junta had not been able to supply the men with uniforms. So the soldiers still wore the different colored outfits which had distinguished the battalions from which they were drawn. For the auxiliary expedition, as it was called, was made up of two companies of Patricios, one of Arribeños, one each of the former Mountaineers and Andalucians, and one of the Castas. (The Arribeños were from the hill provinces, while the Andalucians comprised the one Spanish regiment in favor of the revolution.) To these were added 50 soldiers from the Fijo—the old Viceregal guard—and 50 from the Dragoons and Hussars, as well as

100 lancers. The Patricios wore blue jackets and helmets with blue and white plumes. The Arribeños sported red and black helmets and scarlet lapels. And the provincial Mountaineers wore bright red jackets with red plumes on their helmets, while some of the Indian troops appeared in blue jackets with yellow lapels.[14] A motley band it was, stretched out like a gaudy rainbow. The army of the Patria!

The honor of leading this army had been given to Colonel Ocampo, accompanied by a major staff composed of Vieytes, Chiclana, and Vicente López, and with Colonel Balcarce as second in command.

From the beginning Moreno wrote instructions for the conduct and progress of the expedition. In the directions for the staff which he wrote on June 16, he said:

> The members of the army Junta should procure the greatest possible harmony, it being necessary that virtue distinguishes our soldiers from conquerors who are instruments of ambition or greed. Take special care to remit with all safety the person of Santiago Liniers. The expedition should wait four leagues outside of Córdoba, intimating to the Governor and Cabildo that they should let the people work freely in the election of their deputies. For this purpose the Governor should leave the city during the election. If the Governor resists this, the troops will move against him, first issuing a proclamation to the people that we come not to attack but to defend them, and warning the Governor that he will pay with his blood and possessions for what he causes the vassals of the king to lose.[15]

Here Moreno is still using the "mask" of loyalty to Ferdinand, as indeed he had to, so long as the Junta was insecure and might need the help of the British.

The different regiments of the auxiliary expedition, while composed of an odd assortment of men, were led by brave and intelligent officers. Although Ocampo, the Colonel in charge, was to prove a disappointment and to care more for ostentation than for fighting, Balcarce was a real leader. Among the other heads of regiments who stood out were Viamonte, Díaz Velez, and Martín Rodríguez, "youths of the first families of Buenos Aires." [16] Most important, they were devoted to the cause of independence. As we have seen, Martín Rodríguez, chief of the Arribeños, had already figured prominently in the *Club of the Seven*, and had been most insistent that the trick played by Leiva and the Cabildo, in choosing first a Junta headed by the Viceroy, should be resisted. All the same Moreno knew that this expedition which he was sending to woo the interior towns away from the plots of Liniers and his associates was a bold gamble.

He pursued the expedition with directives and letters, like an anxious parent following each step of a young son who has left home for the first time. In his patrol decree, following the attack on Judge Caspe, he had said, "We have consecrated ourselves to your welfare, and we will die to achieve it." In following the expedition with his orders he was doing just that. He knew he could not let the project fail.

Simultaneously with his directions to the soldiers, Moreno sent circulars to the authorities of the interior towns, asking them to be ready to receive this expedition of 1,000 men, which, he said, would soon be doubled.[17] He also notified these officials that the reactionary chiefs of Córdoba were under arrest, and that one of the objects of the expedition was to capture them and send them back to Buenos Aires for trial. Since he feared that Liniers and the others would try to make their escape he wanted the interior officials to waylay and hold them until the expedition could take over.

From July 13 on he wrote every three days or so to this

expeditionary force.[18] Late in June he had received a note from the Córdoban Cabildo which not only annulled its first adhesion to the Junta but at the same time dared the Buenos Aires government to send forth its army.[19] (This note was the result of a meeting between Governor Concha and Santiago Liniers, together with members of the Cabildo of Córdoba.) Strangely enough Córdoba had taken such action despite the fact that the creoles, supposedly, had a sympathizer in the Cabildo there by the name of Gregorio Funes.

Funes, who was a Dean of the church, was the brother of one of Moreno's former clients. Mariano knew the family well enough to realize that their adhesion to the Junta was less through conviction than through personal spite towards men on the other side. At any moment, if the chances for advancement which Dean Funes awaited might seem good with the Spaniards, or if their cause should look more popular, then the Dean might be persuaded to waver. In any event he would probably try to play both sides of the fence, as Saavedra had appeared to do in the early days of May.

On July 16, Moreno wrote the army precise instructions to insure the imprisonment of the rebels, and told them to do so without listening to Funes, the rebels' relatives, or anyone else.

> Do it in spite of difficulties, nor flatter yourselves with hopes or promises for greater benefits, without effecting. . . at all risks the imprisonment of these men and their remission to Buenos Aires, notifying us by a messenger of their arrival so that the Junta may take convenient precautions.[20]

Meanwhile the counterrevolutionary leaders in Córdoba had sent instructions to all the towns dependent on the Intendency of Córdoba, ordering them not to send delegates to the Buenos Aires Congress. News of this countermand reached the Junta through the Mendoza Cabildo, which wrote of how it had been intimidated by messages from Liniers and Concha. Intimidation had come early, in fact, with an order from Córdoba's governor, Concha, for the town of Mendoza to send him troops. Mendoza had replied that this was impossible, since the city would then be left defenseless in case of an Indian attack. Yet one of the town's military chieftains, a royalist sympathizer named Ansay, had assaulted the barracks one night, stolen arms, and taken with him 200 men to assist the Córdoban leaders. Moreno had to act quickly and he did so by sending at once an agent from the Junta to Mendoza. Soon afterwards he received word from his agent, Moron, that because of Ansay's act the people had gathered at six o'clock the next morning in Cabildo and resolved to oppose Córdoba and defend the Junta to the last drop of their blood.[21]

Mariano was writing further directions in his office in the fort when he received this news. Since it was a cold night in July he was wearing a white woolen scarf around his neck—a striking contrast to his dark hair and eyes. As usual, Manuel worked at the desk nearby. They had been almost ready to start home when the young messenger arrived, handing Mariano the note.

Mariano clapped his hands on the boy's shoulders.

"*Bravo y perfecto!*" he cried, handing the message to Manuel.

"Good. Great. Yes." Manuel laughed. "But your eyes are shooting sparks of fire, Mariano. What have you got up your sleeve, *hombre?*"

"The *Gaceta.*" Moreno's face shone with its special radiance. "Don't you see? It's a perfect story for the *Gaceta*—what Mendoza has done. Listen to this. Did you read where Mendoza mentions among its reasons for support of us how it should be evident, but wasn't to those royalists, that a laboring people whose products are the only basis of their subsistence have no other exportation or place of sale except the Capital! With which they alone maintain commercial relations! Manuel—the owners of the wine shops in the street of Mendocinos—they'll love it."

"Of course. You and the Junta lowered district duties between us and Mendoza and it's bearing fruit."

"*Cierto*. We'll publish the whole thing. Their oath to defy Córdoba and defend us. Everything. Our people need the boost, Manuel. We've got it now. We've got it and we'll give it to them!"

On July 9 everyone on the street was clamoring for this *Gaceta* which contained the Mendoza Cabildo's reply to Concha. At the same time Moreno sent the auxiliary expedition a copy of the correspondence and wrote a stirring note of congratulation to Mendoza. Buenos Aires took on new hope and zest for the struggles to come.

With all his duties as a one-man cabinet, Moreno's diplomacy might easily have given way these days. For the time being, however, it did not. Nor could it. Since the very existence of the Junta depended on his genius, the other members gave him his hand.

Now, as more news kept coming in of the plots in Córdoba, his notes to the expedition wending its way northward became crisper and firmer. In his note of July 19 to the army, in which he sent copies of Mendoza's correspondence with Córdoba, he wrote:

> These copies are sent with due reserve, emphasizing the importance of the principal object of the expedition, for with...an exemplary punishment exercised on the leaders [of Córdoba] the other chiefs will be afraid and

the people will act without the coercion and violence they now suffer.[22]

On July 27 he sent another note to the army, still insisting on the need to send the Córdoban leaders to Buenos Aires. But one day later he dispatched a different and a stronger order.

News had come of the meeting of a War Junta in Córdoba, where the members had given the Governor the right to dispose of the public funds, amounting to more than 76,000 pesos, in order to resist the Buenos Aires expedition and try to disrupt it with bribes. One man had even been promised 58,000 pesos to mix with the expeditionary troops, set fire to their ammunition wagons, and blow them to pieces.

Moreno received news of these schemes in letters intercepted by his scouts, one of whom was the famous gaucho and future General, Martín Güemes. He brought these notices to an extraordinary session of the Junta. He then asked for a vote on whether the Córdoban leaders should be condemned to death by court-martial. With the exception of the priest, Alberti, who abstained, the men voted unanimously in favor of the death sentence. Moreno's next note to the army, on July 28, ordered the head of the expedition to capture the leaders of the counterrevolution at once and put them to death.[23]

Will the expedition carry out his order? Unfortunately Ocampo, still dazzled by the glamour of the former French Viceroy, Liniers, was vacillating.

In some of the intercepted letters brought to him, Moreno had seen evidence that Concha, acting for Liniers, was corresponding with sympathizers in Buenos Aires. If Liniers should be brought to the Capital, upon his arrival there would be attempts to smuggle him over to Montevideo to lead an army against the Junta. The days looked dark, indeed, until these leaders could be captured and put to death.

For Mariano there was no hesitation as to what to do. He would write the expedition again. Only one question remained: Would the army carry out the order in time?

XII

Moreno's Guidance of the Auxiliary Expedition to the Interior; Repulse of Spanish Attempts at Blockade

"... we can affirm that the former government had, indeed, condemned us to vegetate in obscurity and depression, but that, as nature has created us to do great things, we have begun to do them!"
Moreno, Mariano, *Impugnación de Un Bando del Virrey de Lima*, in *Doctrina Democrática de Mariano Moreno*, edited by Ricardo Rojas, p. 198.

Moreno's exasperation reached its height when he received news that, upon the expedition's arrival outside Córdoba, the counterrevolutionary leaders had escaped. Hints of this possibility had come to him a few days before with a message from Ocampo asking that the death sentence for these men should not be carried out, since Funes was pleading with him to suspend it. Such hints, of course, only aggravated the news of the leaders' escape.

Moreno might well have been irritated. Had he not warned Ocampo earlier not to listen to Funes? Meanwhile the message came that the leaders had been captured, at last, by Balcarce. Should he insist, again, upon the death sentence? Would Colonel Balcarce also vacillate?

Once again Moreno called the Junta into special session. He reiterated how the life of the new government was hanging in the balance. The members discussed the alternatives to court-martial. What about sending Liniers into exile instead? Impossible, when exit from the port was impeded by Montevideo's blockading squadron. Imprisonment then? But where was there a prison from which the counter-revolutionaries could not escape?

As the discussion continues in the Junta's meeting-room Mariano walks back and forth, measuring his thoughts with his steps, measuring the risk of firmness, of summary execution, with the greater risk of temporization. Persuasion, he tells himself, has been tried before and failed. No, it must be—it has to be—court-martial. "Court-martial!" he decides. The others agree.

The Junta discusses sending Castelli with Rodríguez Peña as his Secretary to join Balcarce in *Cabeza del Tigre* and see that the court-martial is carried out. One of the men says:

"But what if Castelli becomes weak like our General?"

All at once Moreno turns to Larrea. "If Castelli should falter, then Larrea will go, whom, I believe, to be of sufficient resolution." [1]

Silence. All eyes turn on Mariano. The men, the embryo nation, freedom itself are there before him, ready to be discarded or molded into reality through his ability for decision, for the last act of sacrifice. The decision comes like a flash.

"If necessary, in the end, I shall go myself!"

Castelli left on his mission without wavering.

Then Moreno answered Ocampo's vacillation with a blistering note:

> Obedience is the first virtue of a general and the best lesson he should give to his army of what he must exact in the act of combat. The Superior Government gathers and ponders matters which cannot be communicated and which the executors do not need to know in order to fulfill punctually their orders.[2]

Finally, on August 26, the leaders of Córdoba, among them the famous Liniers, were executed under a court-martial conducted by Castelli and Peña and Balcarce. It was shortly afterwards that Moreno ordered Balcarce to replace Ocampo as commander of the expedition.

Buenos Aires could breathe a little more freely now, and Moreno could find a few more "in between" moments to write articles for the *Gaceta*. He was planning to publish a reprint of a Spanish translation of Rousseau's *Social Contract*. But before doing so he wanted to give the people news of the fate of the expedition and the events taking place in other parts of the Viceroyalty and throughout Spanish America. In his mind, the Buenos Aires movement should serve as a spearhead of freedom for all the colonies. The resistance just beginning to be announced from the Viceroy of Lima made this fact, indeed, inescapable.

Luckily for the movement for independence of the Spanish colonies Moreno, himself, was at the same time becoming transformed. The scholarly, religious and diplomatic lawyer, the recluse who had only become daring before in moments when his legal services were needed for defense of the weak, this Moreno now began to change with a lightning-like release of energy. With uncanny intuition he realized that he could not escape one of two courses. Either he could burn himself out in forming free men to realize the revolution, or he could go slowly, as too many others, including Saavedra, were anxious to do, and let the whole movement for independence fizzle to ashes. Being Moreno, he chose the former course. From now on he became at once a whirlwind of executive orders (some of them petulant) and a whiplash of sarcasm and reason.

While Saavedra rode in the Viceregal carriage, Moreno walked briskly back and forth to his office in the fortress palace three times a day. He wore the same simple lawyer's suit of black that he had always worn. Only Maria may have seen that the broad white stock, folded through his collar with an elaborate twist, was more perfectly starched than before. Except for the concentrated, wrapt expression on his face, as he worded one of his articles while he walked, one could hardly distinguish him from anyone else. Many times, however, he was alive to the people around him, and spoke to them with light in his expression and that sparkle in his eye which so endeared him to his friends. Lately, however, he was more absorbed than receptive, quicker in his walk, more ironical in his expression.

Brother Cayetano prayed for him with real anxiety during this period. Yet it is doubtful if he ever tried to caution his former pupil.[3]

After the execution of Liniers, Moreno's fierce support of his ideals and of the Junta's position stand out more and more. From now on his acts are a continuous response to the intensified threats against Buenos Aires. Unfortunately, too, he is having to work more and more alone. During the last few weeks he had been forced to send many of his colleagues into other parts of the Viceroyalty. The reason was to be found in the desperate calls for help that poured in from the interior towns. There was much less experience in freedom of expression there than in the North American colonies where the colonists had been schooled, even before their independence, in many facets of self-government through frequent town meetings and popularly elected colonial assemblies. As the towns of the Viceroyalty began to hold Cabildo meetings for discussion of support of the Junta, the subsequent upheavals in the old way of life and system of government was causing a confusion which was badly in need of guidance. To supply it Moreno sent them some of the best men from the old *Club of the Seven.*

The Junta, of course, could hardly spare these men. But Moreno knew how desperately they were needed in the key towns. And so he sent Chiclana to Salta, Pueyrredón to Córdoba as governor to replace Concha, and Castelli to Potosí. Formerly Paso had been spared from his job of Secretary of the Treasury to go to Montevideo and speak there before the Open Cabildo meeting, urging unity with and support for the Junta. But Montevideo, under Governor Soria, who had replaced Elío, was still under the dominant sway of the peninsular Spaniards, two of whose warships were waiting conveniently in her harbor. No wonder that Paso's mission failed. After his return, the menace from this quarter, as well as from Paraguay, further north, became intensified. It was going to be necessary soon to send an army against them under Belgrano—another member of the Junta who would have to leave Buenos Aires and who could least of all be spared.

As we have seen, Azcuénaga, still another member of the Junta, was busy running the munitions factory and training troops in Buenos Aires, while Larrea, one of the two Spaniards in the government and one of the wealthiest members, was occupied, with Paso, in raising and allocating funds. This left Moreno particularly alone in the executive field, except for the help he might receive from the other Spaniard, Matheu, from the priest, Alberti, and from the lukewarm President Saavedra. By now, however, he had become an expert organizer as well as creative thinker—

qualities which are reflected in his actions, letters and articles that are henceforth clearer, as well as more forceful.

As soon as he knew that Liniers had been captured, Moreno had looked to the next object of the expeditionary force. In the far northwest the Viceroy of Lima was threatening aggression against the pitifully small patriot army, trying to engage against it the forces of Quito and of the towns further south: those of La Paz and Cochabamba, and, south of them, the troops of Chuquisaca and Potosí. Chuquisaca, Potosí, and La Paz, ruled since their abortive revolutions earlier by the Spaniards Nieto, Sanz, and Goyeneche, could raise a powerful force. This Moreno knew he must prevent. The success of the expedition would depend on guerrilla tactics and surprise attacks. He, himself, must direct this strategy, and he wrote to the army:

> It being one of the principal objects of the expedition to surprise the towns of Peru before reinforcements from Lima can put them in a state of vigorous defense, it would be... convenient that a division of 500 men advance to Tupiza to stay until the arrival of the greater part of the army.[4]

Tupiza was just south of Chuquisaca and the pass between Suipacha and Tupiza was the place where Nieto had written Concha that he would destroy the Junta's army. Moreno wanted to surprise and cut off this attack. He went on to say:

> The distance from Potosí to Tupiza would prevent this division being attacked, if precautions and fortifications... are made. The agitation of the Governors, seeing menace so near, would confuse their plans and encourage the peoples. But a possible rout of the vanguard would be serious, so I only suggest this plan and leave its execution up to the patriotism of the army staff.[5]

One senses the immense difficulties under which he was working in this appeal to patriotism, both pathetic from the

point of view that his army was so small, and daring in its
conception of surprise for an enemy of much greater force.
As news came later from Pueyrredón about desertions in
the patriot army, Moreno's letters become even more remarkable for their patient insistence on discipline, on keeping clear the Junta's goal — an insistence which would reap
benefits later.

On September 22, he wrote the army staff:

> The unwise measure of keeping those troops in the
> city of Córdoba and the little zeal towards discipline
> already foretold the desertion later suffered. The
> greatest rigor toward deserters being an express part of
> the Junta's instructions to the army, this Junta learns
> with sorrow that not one of those guilty of this crime has
> been punished, that impunity has been given to many
> taken prisoner by the Governor of Córdoba [Pueyr-
> redón] and this Junta is without any news about so im-
> portant a matter. And what is worse, without knowledge
> of the fixed number of soldiers composing this army.[6]

He went on to emphasize what he considered the major
defects in discipline. He spoke of officers careless of such
matters as military exercises, and of the first commander's
ignorance of what went on, while the Major Staff declared
honors for itself and treatment of "Captain General,"
"degrading itself with these trivialities (which it has not
sent to the Junta for approval as it should have), and using
time in this way that should have been given to objects of
other importance." He closed with an exhortation to the
zeal and patriotism of the commanders to heed his observations, saying that otherwise the most powerful resource
on which the great work of the Junta had counted would
crumble.

That Moreno, himself, never lost faith, in view of these
discouraging reports, is remarkable. Instead of temporiz-
ing, he pursued his work with even greater zeal. True, he

was receiving encouragement from other quarters, for Santiago del Estero, Tucumán, and Salta sent pledges of allegiance to the Junta, with the news that they were training troops to join the patriot army.[7]

As a result of Moreno's firmness in the note of September 22, Balcarce advanced with the expeditionary army to Salta, leaving Ocampo in Santiago del Estero to organize reinforcements. While this was going on, the reactionaries of Chuquisaca and Potosí, who were waiting for the columns of Liniers and Concha to join them, learned that these leaders had been executed. At the same time a creole revolt broke out in Quito north of Lima, thus diverting the royalist troops of the Viceroy Abascal. And then, suddenly, the most encouraging news of all came to Buenos Aires. Upon the approach of the patriot army, Cochabamba—strategically located between La Paz and Chuquisaca—threw out its royalist officials and installed a government favorable to the Junta.[8] With this assurance of a friendly country through which to march, the expedition could proceed more easily to the rather risky and bold strategy which Moreno had outlined: the plan to surprise the Peruvian armies near Tupiza before reinforcements could reach them.

While the situation outside of Buenos Aires was thus a mixture of hope and incertitude, the fate of the new government inside the city was still precarious. The Junta had received news that Montevideo was asking aid of the Portuguese in Brazil to blockade the port. On top of that, Moreno learned that the members of the Buenos Aires Cabildo, in ironic contrast to the recent patriot adherence of adjacent interior towns, had secretly sworn to the Council of Regency in Spain. He had noticed, of course, that they had not held meetings for some time and that their whole attitude was suspicious and insulting. It was now obvious that they were plotting with Montevideo to overturn the Junta, which they had sworn so recently to uphold. Moreno brought evidence of their treason to a special session of the government. He asked that a vote be taken on sending the men into exile. As a result, the Junta voted to deport the *Cabildantes* to various parts of the Viceroyalty, with the order that they could not return to Buenos Aires for six years.[9]

Ten days later President Saavedra wrote to Feliciano Chiclana, who was now in Potosí, telling him of the deportation of the councilmen and of their treason. "Their crime was doubtless greater than that of the little leaders of Córdoba," he wrote. "Never could I have imagined such deceit. I assure you that this event is very painful and that only justice could have moved me to defy them completely, so that our concept of fairness and impartiality would not fail." [10]

From this statement by the always lukewarm Saavedra it is evident that Moreno knew how to carry the people with him against all tendencies toward a reaction in favor of Spain. Sensing that ridicule, coupled with logic, could be a powerful weapon to cement the popular will to resist the old authorities, he used his powers of sarcasm and learning to the hilt. He used them not only against Nieto—cocky inspector of troops whom Cisneros had sent to Chuquisaca—but also against the Spanish ambassador in Río de Janeiro, Casa–Irujo,[11] and, later, the Viceroy Abascal of Lima. And he published these articles, bristling with epithets, in the *Gaceta.* He was becoming the Thomas Paine, as well as the chief executive, of the Argentine revolution.

Nieto had written insulting words about the patriot expedition, which he said he would destroy. Writing in the *Gaceta*, Moreno recalled how Nieto had acted when he first came to Buenos Aires with the Viceroy Cisneros and knew that he was to lead an army of Patricios (native patriot troops) to crush the revolt in Chuquisaca:

> Animated with the hope of pillage, in the joy on his face could be discovered the plans of thefts, bribes, sales of offices. . .and other plots typical of his character and of the insatiable hunger expected of a man who began to command at eighty and had set foot on America without a single brass coin. If the hostilities of the martinets continue, equally will continue the expedition, which will free the Peruvian patriots of the oppression they suffer, and, purging Peru of some great monsters that infest it, will be called by our sons the expedition of Theseus.[12]

When Casa–Irujo, Spanish ambassador in Río de Janeiro, sent Buenos Aires a proclamation "addressed to the Spanish inhabitants of 'America Meridional', " urging them to reinstate the Viceroy Cisneros and, in case Buenos Aires resisted, to incite all the other towns of the Viceroyalty to crush this resistance, Moreno published a paraphrase of his proclamation in the *Gaceta*, and then answered it.

> The people of America will certainly be surprised that the Marqués directs proclamations to them from a foreign court. (He was purposely playing up this Portuguese angle, for he knew how the Spanish colonists had a tradition of conflict with the Portuguese.) And they will also be surprised that, with an imposing tone, he dictates rules of conduct to provinces never dependent on him. . . . The Marqués and his chiefs. . . tremble lest America arrive at a constitution for herself and in the positive exclusion they make of any other party prove their adhesion to only one, which is to follow the fate of the Peninsula if it remains subject to the domination that threatens. . . . We do not believe the soul of the Marqués is led by an immoderate desire to preserve the windmills of. . . . Cádiz; but we know very well that nothing could happen more contrary to his ideas than the establishment of this new government. The peoples think freely about. . . their rights and are consulted

about them...; they discuss their duties, and learn
quickly that never will they give greater proofs of their
fidelity than when they shake off all danger of seeing
themselves involved in the domination of Joseph Bonaparte.... When the Marqués had not meditated the sad
consequences of his conduct, he should have feared at
least lest his voice would make no impression on towns
which had never listened to it; he should have wondered
lest the people, not recognizing an echo that had never
sounded in their ears, repeat back and forth to each
other the Spanish adage, 'How does *that* man happen to
be carrying a candle in this funeral?' [13]

The people in general loved a joke like this. Moreno's
ridicule of the Marqués was repeated from table to table in
the cafés and pulperías. In wonder, men remarked how wit-
tily he could hold up the Spanish authorities to scorn, when
from all corners threats kept coming in against the new
government. Somehow he was putting stiffness into their
spines, convincing them of their strength. They were
elated, too, that he had laid bare the falsity of the Marqués's
information that Spain was winning against Napoleon.
Moreno was one to stand up even against the French
Emperor if there were need, people began to say. The valor
of his spirit infected the city and helped make it possible for
Buenos Aires to withstand the mounting danger of attack.

One day the threats came dangerously close. Suddenly
there appeared in the harbor a Spanish warship. Ordering
the other ships to depart, she pointed her guns on the
capital.

The Spaniards in the city grew ecstatic. The Junta, of
course, had no navy. They told themselves that at last
Moreno was trapped. Besides, Caracas was already in the
grip of a Spanish blockade, which the British had not seen
fit to break up, and now here was one of the Spanish ships
from Montevideo imposing a blockade on Buenos Aires.

How false all Moreno's boasts of aid from Lord Strangford in Río de Janeiro in case of such as event! Besides, there was a British officer, Captain Eliot, in the city who was known to be cooperating with the Montevidean blockaders. Probably the ship out there in the harbor had been sent by Casa-Irujo, the Spanish ambassador to Río de Janeiro in order to force a return to the Viceroyalty. Maybe Eliot had promised to help. There were wagers between Spaniards and creoles about how Moreno would have to eat his words. But not for long.

Down there on the shore, washerwomen are screaming as the ship aims its guns and fires. In the market place, people rush for cover, overturning carts and chicken coops and trinket trays. Then, as the people of the Plaza hold their breaths, a strange thing happens.

Two mounted cannon on the parapet of the fortress are being swung into position. Had Moreno given the order? Yes. The next instant a resounding volley rings out. Did he — *Dios*, did he hit the Spanish ship or not? No one can tell. The only thing certain is that the vessel is turning around now. Yes, turning and setting sail out of the harbor! Shouts of joy rise up from the creoles. They might have known it. Moreno is no man to slide around and duck a challenge, as the Viceroy Sobremonte did. He has given shot for shot. And the ship, thank God, the ship is fleeing!

Everyone was praising Moreno on that day in September when he refused to be intimidated by the threat of blockade. Already a party of Morenistas was beginning to spring up.

In a few weeks Moreno explained his actions to the people in the *Gaceta*. This attack by a Spanish ship and the connivance with the attempt by Captain Eliot—who had made no protest against his own ship's being ordered out of the harbor—had been part of the general plan for a blockade fomented by the Spanish Captain Salazar in Montevideo, who had written Casa–Irujo asking him to urge the Portuguese Regent in Brazil to aid the Spanish plans. Moreno knew that the Regent, at the insistence of Lord Strangford, had refused this help since Strangford had protested that the blockade had not been officially proposed by the Spanish government. He also knew that the Prince Regent had pointed out the dangerous consequences of a blockade causing the Junta's army—the strength of which he seems to have overrated—to detour into Paraguay and approach Brazil.[14] On September 25, Moreno, knowing that he had the backing of Lord Strangford, wrote in the *Gaceta*:

> The 21st day of the current month, at 12 o'clock noon, a lateener (of those which the mariners of Montevideo have armed for the blockade of this port) drew near the city, and, after discharging a cannon towards the bluffs in front of Retiro, fled with dispatch.... What cannot be viewed without indignation is the vile attempt to discharge a shot on our shores. Even in wars... rules have been established which lessen the destruction of humanity and only tolerate it insofar as it is conducive to repelling attack or achieving victory.... What was the object of discharging this cannon? Did they think they could frighten us with a shot? Put the city in conflict? Or achieve the run of men who are their enemies only because they don't think in the same way? The shot could have killed a washer-woman, wounded some passerby, and broken some wash tubs. Here is all the result of this feat; nevertheless, the captain of the launch will be praised in the cafes of Montevideo....[15]

There was lively comment about this near disaster, especially after the biting ridicule in Moreno's estimate of the Captain of the attacking launch, who would be praised in Montevideo "since it can't be denied that, in spite of his hasty flight on the first sign of battle, he *was* bold enough to let off at least one cannon shot!'' [16]

Of the conduct of the British Captain, Eliot, he wrote:

> It is unpardonable, the behavior of Eliot, a subordinate official, who broke the trade relations of his nation in the Río de La Plata upon exhortations of a subordinate government like that of Montevideo.... We must separate Eliot's conduct from the generous sentiments of the English.... True it is Lord Strangford does not speak in the public character of his ministry when he shows the Junta personal feelings of a manifest adhesion; but a minister of his rank and accredited talents would not have compromised the safety of his own judgment if he had not believed it guaranteed by the predisposition of his cabinet and the interest of his nation.[17]

Evidence of how Buenos Aires discussed the brave defiance of the blockade and Eliot's connivance with the attackers is shown in the first part of this article:

> With how much vigor has the town expressed itself about the conduct of Eliot relative to the blockade of this Capital! What individual . . . has not taken in this event? Who has not discussed it? [18]

Then Moreno went on to prove further how Eliot's conduct could not have been upheld by England:

> He who observes the political relations of Europe in these times will discover that all of them revolve on no other axis than the reciprocal interest of nations who trade with each other.... Therefore England cannot risk in America any advanced enterprise which, exciting against itself the public spirit of these regions, would leave compromised the union and frank communication with these towns, which so interests that nation. Since the Emperor of the French extended his power over all the coasts of Europe, there were closed to the English nation the principal doors of the immense trade which

forms its richness. It is now necessary for them to open
new canals, which, although they will not entirely make
up for this loss, will somewhat indemnify it, and the vast
continent of America is the only refuge which remains
to the commercial interests of England.

This knowledge has urged the Emperor of the
French to repeated efforts to separate us from all communication with the English. In secret instructions, surprised by our emissaries, he offers a decided protection...in most flattering terms, for the towns of
America if these would close their doors to England and
make her feel the weight of the incommunication which
she suffers in Europe. The risk which these promises in-
cur is very great. He who meditates...the actual state
and true interests of Great Britain will know what great
efforts she must make for the intrigues of France to find
no acceptance in this part of America.... Any English-
man who truly loves his country will have observed with
tenderness the generous resolutions with which the
provinces of the Río de La Plata have dissipated these
dangers.... A general proscription of all the preten-
sions of France, a frank, free commerce with the firm
basis of reciprocal advantages, a friendship for any
English individual resident on this soil, such have been
the measures which England should wish from us and
which we have generously anticipated.[19]

As evidenced above, a new trend was appearing in
Buenos Aires. It grew out of the way Moreno was giving the
people, for the first time, a sense of international trade and
politics, a feeling for the importance they might play in the
relations of nations. In doing so he was showing himself to
be an astute statesman, writing not only for the consumption of the Buenos Aires public, but also for the British,
holding out to them both a warning—in the suggestion of
how Napoleon was courting the colonies—and a promise, in
the reiteration of the trade advantages they could continue
to have only if they supported the Junta government, which

was inimical to the French, as well as to the counter-revolutionary plots of Spanish Viceroys and Governors. He was depending on copies of the *Gaceta* being circulated not only in Buenos Aires where the priests read them to their congregations, but also on their making their way to the British Embassy in Río de Janeiro.

Moreno's letter of protest to Lord Strangford about Eliot and the blockade, together with the protest of several British merchants of Buenos Aires who wished to continue their trade, brought a favorable reply. More than that, Strangford ordered Eliot to leave Buenos Aires and sent Captain Ramsay to see that he carried out the order. But Ramsay accomplished still more. He remained in the city to break up, with his ship the *Misteltoe*, any further attempts at blockade. Now the "liberty of the port, the acquisition of ships and mariners who could take the offensive against the royalist squadron in Montevideo was easy." [20]

Meanwhile, Moreno continued his articles in the *Gaceta*. While some of them were above the heads of the less educated people, there were one or two which contained enough humor to be quoted everywhere. By this time Moreno's witticisms, as well as the frank information which he gave in the *Gaceta*, had become so popular that on Thursdays, the day the weekly paper was printed, large crowds were already standing outside the building which housed the printing press, waiting for copies.

The press had been set up in an annex of the old *Ranchería*, a building with an interesting history. As its name implies, this wooden structure had once been a kind of corral surrounding the thatched huts or *ranchos* of the negro slaves of the Jesuits. It was situated behind the warehouse of the Church of San Ignacio, near the southeast corner of the Plaza Mayor. It was when the Jesuits were expelled in 1767 because of their political activities that the *Ranchería* had been taken over by the state.[21] While its first use by the Viceroys had been as a place to be leased for masked dances, ever since the printing press had been installed there by Vertiz the location was known chiefly as the home of the press. And sometimes, either before or after the publication of the *Gaceta* this block where the press was located was colorfully called "The Block of Knowledge."

Moreno's article ridiculing the declaration of the Viceroy of Lima, who had proclaimed that Buenos Aires should subordinate itself to his rule, was a masterpiece of satire. In it Moreno reminded the people of how Viceroy Abascal had once called Godoy, who had sold out Spain to Napoleon, the "tutelar angel of America." And this same man who had spoken such praise of the traitor Godoy had criticized the Buenos Aires Junta solely because it was composed of creoles, creole Americans who were, the Viceroy said, "men destined by nature to vegetate in obscurity!" Moreno made much of this remark. He wrote:

> This is the last extreme of a senseless arrogance. . . . In our three hundred years of vassalage, the European Spaniard (who stepped on these shores) was noble from his arrival, rich after a few years of residence. . . and puffed up with all the ascendancy given to men who command far from home.
>
> But today the course of human events reduces Spain to slavery, and all the free peoples of the monarchy recover their primitive rights. . . . And since Abascal is so unfortunate in his prophecies as to have those whom he calls 'tutelar angels' converted into demons, we can affirm that the former government had, indeed, condemned us to vegetate in obscurity but that, as nature has created us to do great things, we have begun to do them! [22]

People vied for copies of this article and quotations from it became bywords.

XIII

Moreno's Plans for A Congress to Draw up A Constitution; Publication of Rousseau's Social Contract

"By what means will the Congress achieve the
well-being which is the reason for its having been
called? How can people be urged to view with the
greatest interest what they have always looked on
with indifference? Who will inspire in us that public
spirit which our fathers did not know?.... Who
will give our souls the energy and firmness
necessary for the love of country which has happily
begun to shine among us....?

"...the Laws of the Indies were made for
neophytes ... for a colony [and] we are forming a
state.... But we have no constitution.... Nothing
is more difficult than to fix the principles of an
administration... free from corruption. This is
certainly the first work to which our Congress
should devote itself.... If the powers are balanced,
the purity of the administration will be
maintained."

Moreno, Mariano, *Sobre La Misión del
Congreso* in *Escritos Politicos y Económicos de
Mariano Moreno,* edited by Norberto Piñero, pp.
273, 274, 275, 278.

Moreno—who was to spend more time, later, on his articles for the *Gaceta*—was now giving his greatest attention
to the work of gaining sympathy in other parts of America
for the Buenos Aires government. He had just been able to
secure Lord Strangford's assurances of help against any
further attempt at blockade by Montevideo. Now he wanted
to capitalize on this assurance to win over Chile to the
patriot cause. His correspondence with the Chilean government is further evidence of his skill in the field of foreign affairs.

In answer to the Junta's note of May 28, asking that
Chile recognize the Buenos Aires government, the Chilean
President had stated that, since his Captaincy General was
independent of the Viceroyalty, it must await the resolution
of the Spanish nation in *Cortes* as to events in Buenos Aires,
but that in the meantime all political and commercial relations would continue as before.[1] This was enough encouragement for the Junta to send envoys to Chile to stimulate
secret meetings among the creoles there with the object of
encouraging an independent Junta in Santiago. On
August 30, Moreno answered the Chilean President, saying
that the Buenos Aires movement had come into being with
as much authority as those in Spain, in spite of which the
Peruvian Viceroy, with the aid of Governors Sanz of Potosí
and Nieto of Charcas, had issued a provocative declaration
that the provinces of the Río de La Plata were a part of the
Viceroyalty of Peru. "Since he will doubtless attempt the
same thing against you," Moreno wrote, "we offer you the
chance to share with us in the abundant aid which England
has promised." [2]

At the same time, he wrote the Cabildo of Santiago, ex-
horting it to sustain its rights energetically and to set up its
own government without loss of time. If it could do so immediately, he predicted that "Lima will become doubtful in

the midst of our forces which will enter Peru." [3]

This correspondence, together with the activity of the Buenos Aires agents, began to bear fruit. News soon came of the erection of a Junta in Chile. Moreno gave this news to the *Gaceta* on October 15. The tone of his article showed that, although he did not believe a common or union government to be possible for the two budding nations, he did believe in a vigorous plan of confederation and alliance. This idea of confederation of all Spanish America in an alliance of independent nations, rather than in a federal union (the plan of Miranda and later of Bolívar) was one which Moreno would touch on later in his articles on the *Goals of the Congress.*[4]

It was most encouraging to have Chile, just across the Andes on the west, in the Buenos Aires camp. (Later, when Elío would return to Montevideo as Viceroy and begin preparations to occupy Buenos Aires, Chile would send four hundred soldiers to join the Buenos Aires army.[5]) There were now three independent Juntas in Spanish America, for the one in Caracas was still active, and Caracas, too, would later send Bolívar, after Moreno's death, to meet the counterrevolutionary troops of Peru.

It was just about the time the news came of the installation of the Chilean Junta that the delegates from the different towns to which Moreno had sent circulars began arriving in Buenos Aires. Two of these deputies came from Córdoba, now under the government of the Junta's envoy, Martín de Pueyrredón. These two delegates, both canons of the church, were Dr. Juan Luis de Aguirre and Dean Gregorio Funes — the same Funes against whose advice Mariano had cautioned the head of the expeditionary army in the matter of the capture of Liniers. But Funes, as we have seen, was the type of man to be on the side that was winning. Although he had argued for the release of the counterrevolutionary leaders of Córdoba, he had, at the same time, supported the Junta. Moreno, knowing the man's vanity and his reputation as an erudite canon, decided to ask him, together with Dr. Aguirre, to write some articles for the *Gaceta*.

There was another reason for requesting these articles. From the beginning Moreno had realized that the Roman Catholic Church would pronounce itself against the revolution, and that this must be offset by a government which would serve the Church in strict accordance with the principles and laws of Patronage.[6] All the people who were Catholics, as he himself was, would want to be sure that relations between Church and State were correct. It is true that Mariano had said in his brief defending the Cabildo of Jujuy against the curates of that city:

> There has been...much confusion of the exterior acts of a voluntary cult with the substance of the religion we profess. The exterior cult has no intrinsic relation to the object in which it ends. Now it is an act of worship to bend the knee and tomorrow it could be a sign of mockery or disrespect.[7]

Although he had written these words, he was far from wishing to discard either the substance or the ceremony of the Catholic religion at its best, which he loved. He asked the canons, Aguirre and Funes, therefore, to write articles on the two following propositions: first, whether the Royal Patronage was a privilege connected with sovereignty or with the person of the kings who exercised it; second, whether there existed in the Junta "a legitimate representation of the general will of these provinces," and if so, whether the Junta ought not to rule, instead of some uncertain representative of the captive king.

Aguirre and Funes both answered in articles which upheld the principle that patronage was a privilege of sovereignty, rather than of the kings, and that the Junta had the right to exercise it. For the time being relations between Funes and Moreno remained, at least superficially, cordial.

The degree to which this cordiality was only on the surface would be seen later. For intimacy with the ostentatious Dean, Moreno's character was too democratic and too averse to emphasis on the outward show of religion (so dear to Funes with his hankering after a Bishopric and with the two agents in Madrid whom he kept busy buying him books, music and trinkets).[8] However, the religious issue, never really disturbing, had been settled by Aguirre's and Funes' articles, and Moreno had reason to be grateful.

Meanwhile he had to continue to keep Buenos Aires prepared against invasion and to urge the expeditionary army forward to meet resistance from the north before the counterrevolutionary forces could grow too strong. The tremendous load he was carrying began to make him tired and irritable. His insistence on equality and the merit system and democratic simplicity in government became progressively impatient. He never let up on this insistence. There are many evidences of it in the letters and instructions which he had to write, in such numbers, to Cabildos of the interior, and to temporary governors serving under the Junta.

He wrote to Chiclana, in Salta:

> We must elevate the creoles, make them take an interest in their work, and realize its advantages. You have recommended a certain Echauri to me. But they have told me he does not have a good reputation among the people. *Por Dios, paisano mío*, the people will have only changed from one tyrant to another, if we judge a man by anything but merit and virtue. I withdraw your petition and must punish an insistence on it.[9]

As for his emphasis on simplicity, we remember that

when he replaced the judges of the Buenos Aires *Audiencia* he ordered that the new officials wear only the suits of lawyers. In harmony with this ruling was his letter to the Cabildo of Mendoza, regulating its relations with the Lieutenant Governor, in which he told the Cabildo to "abstain from ceremonious formalities, since this always causes embarrassment in the service." [10] Likewise, in his letter to the Cabildo of Santa Fe, which was delaying its Open Meeting to choose deputies, he wrote "do it without ceremony or special order of seats." [11] Later, in an article for the *Gaceta* of November 1, he criticized the old *Laws of the Indies* bitterly for having dedicated entire chapters to precedence and ceremony.

Moreno had another motive, besides democracy, for his emphasis on simplicity. He particularly wanted to instill more dispatch into the work of the government, and to eliminate the great amount of time which the old colonial officials had wasted in useless ceremony and formality. Besides, he knew that much—perhaps even the very life of the creole government—depended on quick and efficient organization of all resources before the Spaniards could strike. Thus, when Pedro Medrano, whom he had appointed to write instructions to the employees of the Revenue Office, delayed the performance of this duty, Moreno wrote him:

> Promptness should be one of the distinctions of the new government. When the Junta sacrifices every moment, even those necessary for needful repose, to carry out its duties, the other magistrates should also contribute their part, making the people feel the advantages of the new reforms.[12]

Medrano had the conceit to answer:

> Reform should consist rather in firmness, impartiality, judgement and circumspection, and not in the

dangerous speed of expediting business.[13]

Moreno, himself, had been spending even the hours "necessary for needful repose" in sacrifical work for his country. He had tried to teach the people to speak out on their opinions, free of fear, and he was probably glad Medrano felt that he could do so, but after his repeated admonition to the man he had good reason to be exasperated. He replied:

> Have the necessary moderation in your duties and
> the respect with which they should be carried out.[14]

In every department Moreno was trying to expedite the work. Particularly he tried to step up the duties of the *Royal Hacienda* or Treasury Department. To this end he ordered strict observance of Article 217 of the Ordinance for Intendents, which required employees to be in their offices seven hours a day or have their salaries cut, a ruling which had been in force before but never strictly observed.[15] He, himself, was working regular hours from nine to two and five to eight, and going back to the fort after hours to work at night.[16]

Since the government officials had become accustomed to a rather casual and leisurely discharge of their duties, most of them did not relish the change. It was about this time that murmurings against Moreno began to make themselves felt. The discontent, we are told, started with his articles in the *Gaceta, Sobre La Misión del Congreso*, partly because in these articles he began to show clearly that the government should no longer be dependent on Spain. Such clarity consolidated both the peninsular Spaniards and the reactionaries among the creoles against him.

More dangerous, however, was the resentment of some of the young creole cadets and officers against Moreno's

rules for attendance at the *School of Mathematics*, and for
promotion on the basis of merit rather than influence. The
cadets, already possessing commissions, had not relished
the idea of being forced to take a course of at least two
months at the school.[17] And there were impatient, young
hotbloods who did not think it fair that no one could become
an officer unless he went to military school. Another cause
of resentment against these rules stemmed from the fact
that Moreno lacked intimate relations with the military.
Certainly he did not have the same opportunity to know the
men as, for instance, the President Saavedra, who had commanded the patriotic regiment of Patricios ever since the
second English invasion. Always a little irritated by
Moreno, Saavedra soon saw a chance to make use of his
advantage.

In view of the jealousies that were now beginning to be
felt towards Moreno's leadership, his friends begged him to
take an escort or a guard with him when he walked back and
forth to his office in the fort after dark. When they pressed
him, he would quote in Latin, with an arch look of humor
(remembering how, here and there, Saavedra was hinting
that he was a "demon") the following words from Horace:
"When the conscience is pure and the hand free of crime,
there's no need to raise the dart of the Moors, nor the quiver
full of arrows!" [18] At other times he would repeat to his
brother, Manuel, who was the most solicitous for him, the
passage from Cicero that says, "I am ready in any case, for
there is no bad death for the strong, no premature death for
him who has obtained the first honors of his country, no
lamentable death for the wise man." [19] In spite of threats
from the discontented, he resolutely refused a guard. All he
would consent to do was to carry in his pocket a small pistol.

What was the younger Manuel, Mariano's brother, doing during this time? Some Argentines have tried to mini-

mize Moreno's work by saying that it was, in reality, the work of Manuel. But this assertion the brother, himself, never made, and, in fact, nearly all his statements throughout his *Life of Mariano* refute by implication any such idea.

Manuel, who looked up to his brother, helped him in his position as Secretary as we have seen. He recounted that someone in the Junta had proposed his name for an important position in the interior, but that Mariano, true to his principles that no favoritism should be shown his family while he was in office, opposed this suggestion.[20]

"He considered me more useful serving by his side in the Secretaryship," Manuel says, "in the same position that for about ten years I had already carried out." [21] (Even before Mariano's return from Chuquisaca, Manuel had been a government clerk, following in the footsteps of his father.) He has written that Mariano used to tell him that if he had found him among the opponents of the revolution, he would have had no hesitation in applying to him whatever retribution was called for. "And," says Manuel, "I am sure he would have carried out his word. . . . He was the soul of the Junta." [22]

As Mariano, with Manuel to help him, carried on his strenuous work, more and more deputies were arriving from the provincial towns. Their arrival hastened Moreno's resolve to instruct the people in the reasons for which these deputies had come. In his mind the object was very clear. It was to draw up a constitution for governing the land. He had told the different Cabildos of the interior towns about this goal in the second circular which he sent to them, correcting the first note which had simply asked that deputies be sent to Buenos Aires to enter the Junta. Although he had corrected this first wording, the conception of entering the Junta which Dean Funes and Saavedra were planning to uphold was going to be the hardest thing Moreno would have to fight. Time and again he was going to be forced to insist that the Junta was only provisional, and the only excuse for a convocation of deputies to meet in conjunction with the *temporary* Buenos Aires Junta was the drawing up of a democratic constitution.

He started his articles *On the Mission of the Congress* on November 1, even before the expeditionary army had met the forces from Peru. November is spring in Buenos Aires and the weather was beginning to be hot. We can feel some of this heat and impatience in the words with which Moreno announced that he would begin his articles on the mission of the Congress.

The historian, Pablo Groussac, has implied that Moreno's energy sprang from a highly nervous temperament. He speaks of Moreno's irritable character and exasperated energy as evidence of something that was morbid and convulsive, which produced a "frightening activity." [23] There is some indication of a fanatic and compulsive energy in Mariano in these days of crisis, when the army he directed with his pen still had to meet its first, severe test, and when his own government was showing signs of vacillation about calling the Congress and writing the constitution that was so needed. With Moreno—as with Churchill in England's darkest hour—crisis and the will to face it had met. As the type of struggle each man was called upon to face was different, so were the men. The Napoleonic menace of 1810, with its chance for freedom for Spain's colonies, demanded and produced a "colonist" whose nervous energy was entirely devoted to the ideal of lifting up a whole people out of apathy into self-realization.

Moreno had held back from this dream of his boyhood, this inner urge for service to his people, until others made the revolution inevitable. Then, once the challenge was presented to him, he took it so fully that his activity in the cause was "frightening" only because of the difference in the clarity of his perception and that of the lesser men around him. His "sickness" was merely the dedication which all normally selfish men call a malady.

At this time he wanted to start the deputies discussing the constitution among themselves, so that they would be ready with constructive ideas for the Congress which would convene as soon as all of them had arrived. He wrote:

> The scorn of the wise and the hatred of peoples will perpetuate into... opprobium those who, ill-using moments not to be repeated for many centuries, cheat the hopes of their fellow citizens. I incite you then, respectable individuals of our Congress... work with the conviction that the successive benedictions of a thousand generations will honor your memory.[24]

Later he said:

> I will speak on all the points I have proposed. I will not preserve any order in their arrangement, because I wish to avoid the presumption... that a systematic work was intended. I will prefer in each *Gaceta* the question which first comes to my mind.[25]

This frank statement of the way he was having to write is an indication of the tremendous pressure under which he was working. He had asked all the deputies to write their own ideas on constitutional organization and publish them side by side with his. Only Funes responded to this request.[26]

Meanwhile, Moreno was following the progress of the expeditionary army. Earlier he had already worked out a plan of campaign, and had written the leaders advising them to send an advance detachment to the pass between Suipacha and Tupiza with which to surprise the counter-revolutionary forces. He was even more concerned with the political administration of the towns and provinces which would come over to the Junta as a result of the expedition's progress. We have seen that he and the Junta had sent Castelli earlier to join the expedition in order to conduct the court-martial of Liniers and his adherents. It is to Castelli that he now turned for further aid, naming him a director of army movements and an organizer of government in the towns. The instructions to Castelli were signed by Azcuénaga, with additions by Moreno, and were entitled "Instructions to be Observed by the Representative of the Junta, Dr. Don Juan José Castelli, in the Government of the Expedition to the Interior Provinces Which Has Been Entrusted to Him." [27]

It should be noted that these instructions were issued after the Junta had received news of desertions among the patriot troops. Also, the blockade by Montevideo's squadron was constantly threatening, and had not yet been broken up entirely by Lord Strangford's intervention. In addition, preparations were now being made in Buenos Aires to send reinforcements to Belgrano's army, which was meeting more resistance than had been expected from Paraguay. Thus the instructions to Castelli contain, in places, a rather ruthless note. Castelli is advised that in the first victory he should let the soldiers ravage the neighborhood in order to instill fear. He is also instructed to execute the counterrevolutionary leaders Nieto, Sanz, Goyeneche, and the Bishop Orellana of La Paz in whatever place they may be captured. Moreno also added that, in the towns passed through, all Cabildo members who did not support the revolution should be sent to Buenos Aires. Only the priest, Alberti, signed in dissent against this decision.[28]

By this time Balcarce was heading the expedition, while the former commander, Ocampo, was remaining in Santiago del Estero to organize reinforcements.[29] Due to Moreno's insistence, Balcarce was advancing steadily north. His advance suffered, however, from lack of mules to carry provisions. Nevertheless, the counterrevolutionary leaders were worried at news of the advance. Sanz, in Potosí, began writing to Nieto for reinforcements. Nieto, in turn, asked help from Goyeneche. The Viceroy Abascal of Lima promised aid, and started to send a force under Colonel Ramirez to stop the Junta's army at Tupiza. At this moment, however, Cochabama rose up in favor of the revolution and prevented Ramirez from marching south to join Nieto's forces. The situation looked especially favorable for Balcarce to follow Moreno's suggestions for a surprise advance.

Meanwhile the royalist Captain Córdoba, in charge of Nieto's troops, had retreated to Cotagaita, behind the Cotagaita river, and about 20 leagues behind his first encampment at Tupiza.[30] Balcarce decided to move as fast as possible to attack the enemy at Cotagaita. He outdistanced his supplies, and found that he could not even let his horses drink from the river without being fired on by the enemy, lined up 2,000 strong, on the opposite shore. As Balcarce had already sent the gaucho Güemes back to Salta for reinforcements and mules and horses, he decided to retreat to Tupiza and await supplies from Güemes. But since Tupiza was too open a place to be easily defended, and since he still needed some artillery and munitions which had not yet caught up with him, he continued to retreat with the royalists in pursuit and did not stop until he reached the river Suipacha. On the seventh of November Captain Córdoba attacked. Balcarce, having by this time fortified his center, feigned a hurried retreat. As the counterrevolutionaries advanced in disorder, Balcarce's army rallied and charged them in a headlong encounter. They completely routed the royalists.[31] News of the victory of Suipacha electrified Buenos Aires.

Before Moreno learned of it, and right after he had received word about the retreat from Cotagaita, he wrote Castelli saying that the Junta confided in his reorganization of the army and that it approved the "system of blood and rigor" which Castelli had proposed against the Junta's enemies.[32] These words were later used against Moreno in support of the contention that he was Robespierian in his methods, but the fact remains that both in this communication of November 18 and a later one of December 3, after the news of the victory had reached him, he also wrote Castelli to make himself "loved" by the natives of Potosí "with gentleness of treatment." [33]

In his second letter Moreno ordered that a general pardon be published for all enemy officers and soldiers who would lay down their arms and obey the new government. (Before this it should be noted that in reply to a request from Pueyrredón that the children of one of the counter-revolutionary leaders of Córdoba, who had been executed, should be cared for, Moreno had written instructions to assign to these children three hundred pesos annually from the branch of vacant "majors and minors." The amazing thing is that he should have made time to attend to such details as the money for these orphans.) Pueyrredón soon wrote him that Córdoba was convinced its new government was just, and that many had reason to bless it as a true benefactor. Now, however, Moreno also emphasized to Castelli the Junta's desire that there should not remain in Peru any European soldier or citizen who had taken arms against the Capital.

As the high pitch of excitement over Balcarce's victory began to subside a little, a feeling started to grow among the more cautious element that Moreno was too harsh to the Spaniards. Not everyone had approved of the execution of Liniers and his followers, nor did everyone approve the execution of Nieto and Captain Córdoba, which took place on December 15, followed later by the execution of Paula Sanz, Governor of Potosí. Yet Sanz, a protégé of Godoy's, who had been run out of Buenos Aires years before on a conviction of fraud, had been a cruel governor. He was one of the men who was particularly merciless towards the Indians, in the way he used them in *mitas* to work the mines—those *mitas* which Moreno had argued against while he was at the University of Chuquisaca. As we remember he had said "it is better to conserve the life of mortals than of metals!" [34] But Sanz had continued to defy the precautionary rules for safeguarding the Indians' health in a scandalous manner. And there was evidence that he had governed the creoles with equal cruelty.

It was for these reasons that the Junta published a *Manifesto* explaining the need for sentencing these men to death and showing additional evidence that the counterrevolutionary leaders had plotted execution of the members of the Junta.[35] Moreno's article on the patriotic uprising of Cochabama also appeared about this time. In this article he showed his enthusiasm for equality between the different towns under the new government. He said that Cochabamba had competed in glory and heroism with the Capital and that the inhabitants of Cochabama, "equalling our valor, will also equal our influence." [36]

At the moment none of this could quell the discontent at the Secretary's attitude towards the Spaniards, not only of the interior but also of Buenos Aires. Even some creoles were willing to overlook the Spaniards' grumbling, to countenance their desire for a return to the old order, and to think not too harshly of their plots. All this caused Moreno to work harder than ever to make the revolution survive.

At the same time he did not want the new government

to be a military one, and he deplored the fact that so much emphasis had to be placed on the training of soldiers. He hoped to counteract the tendency towards militarism by the foundation of such institutions as the public library. In the article announcing the opening of the library he had written:

> Peoples buy at a... high price the glory of arms, and the blood of citizens is not the only sacrifice which accompanies triumphs: the Muses, terrified... flee... and men, insensible to all that is not... violence, neglect those establishments which in happy times are founded for the cultivation of the sciences and arts. If the magistrate does not employ his power and zeal to prevent the fatal end to which so dangerous a condition progressively leads, then the ferocity of a barbaric people will take the place of gentility, and the rudeness of the sons will dishonor the memory of the great actions of the fathers.
>
> Buenos Aires is menaced with so terrible a fate; four years of glory in warfare (against the British and now against the Spanish royalists) have undermined the intelligence and virtue which produced them. Necessity forced the College of San Carlos to be destined temporarily for barracks for the troops. Young people began to enjoy a liberty as dangerous as it was agreeable... they wanted to be soldiers before preparing themselves to be men. Everyone has viewed with sorrow those establishments destroyed for the education of our young people, and good patriots lament the... disastrous policies (of the former government) which viewed as an evil of dangerous consequesces the education of the people.
>
> The Junta saw itself reduced to the sad necessity of creating everything; and all the grave matters which crowded in did not leave it the time it desired to consecrate to so important an object. It will call to its aid wise and patriotic men who, ruling over a new establishment of studies... will form the educational institution which

will produce, someday, men who are the honor and glory
of their patria.

While this work is being organized... the Junta has
resolved to form a public library, in which is faciliated to
lovers of letters a sure means of augmenting their
knowledge.[37]

He went on to say that the library had enough books to
start with, but that he would welcome donations for
building shelves and defrayment of other expenses. He
named Brother Cayetano Rodríguez one of the two Directors of the Library, the same Cayetano in whose Franciscan
library he had read his first books on freedom and democracy. With what poetic justice, then, did the ardent, gentle
friar now take his place as head of that public library which
would help "form the men" for whom he had prayed long
ago!

While outstanding creoles were receiving important
posts under the new government, the Spaniards felt more
and more that they were being discriminated against. "It
was no secret within the Junta, nor was it one without, that
Moreno had become the Director of the Revolution. The
public knew by instinct that everything accomplished was
done through his inspiration. Internal politics were the
result of his plans, and foreign relations were in his hands.
The Naval Commander Salazar, in Montevideo, informed
his superiors by condensing his judgement in these words,
'Moreno is the first man in the Junta and the first terrorist.' " [38]

"Terrorist" and "Jacobin" were handy words to use
against him at this time, when the horrors of the French
revolution were still vivid memories. Starting in November,
when Mariano began publishing his articles about the Congress showing that he contemplated real independence
from Spain and not just a government to uphold the rights

of the captive King Ferdinand, the threats against him began to multiply. Soon they invaded his home.

Maria was terrified. And well she might be. Someone hurled through the window, near which she was sewing, a note announcing her husband's approaching death.

XIV

Exile and Death

"I hope that someday I shall enjoy the gratitude of those who are now against me, but whom I pardon with all my heart, and whose erring conduct I view even with a certain kind of pleasure. For I prefer to the interest of my own credit that the people begin to think about their government, although they commit errors which they will later correct."

Moreno, Mariano — Words of his resignation from the government, in *La Revolución de Mayo y Mariano Moreno*, by Ricardo Levene, p. 300.

Colonel Saavedra had been jealous of Moreno from the start. In a letter he wrote to Feliciano Chiclana in 1811, he spoke of how he had triumphed over Mariano by crushing Alzaga's attempt at revolt on January 1, 1809. Moreno, of course, played only a small part in this uprising. He had warned Alzaga, we remember, against any kind of government which did not include creoles. Still Saavedra spoke of how Moreno, envious of his position, was always trying to get revenge for the trick he, Saavedra, had played on him on that day.[1] The idea that Moreno, in the midst of his almost crushing work, could have spared a moment to think back on his part in the January 1 incident, into which he had only halfheartedly entered, is obviously ridiculous and at the least extremely doubtful. That Saavedra could have taken his own role on that day, in relation to Mariano's, so seriously, is intimation enough that if anyone were jealous, it was the President himself.

To Saavedra, unimaginative and, for the time being, almost useless as far as the progress of the revolution was concerned, there remained plenty of time for brooding. Even with all the apparatus of the former Viceroys at his command—the coach, the escort, the lackeys, the seat of preference at every ceremony—with all this and his title of President, he was so much less than Moreno in the revolution that the fact had begun to eat on him. Little wonder then that his mind dwelled on the past, when he had been something more.

From the very first, as we have noted, Saavedra appears not to have grasped the full significance of the revolution. Greater freedom, a government which would be the voice of the governed, equal opportunity for education, promotion of position based on merit rather than influence— these things seemed at best, to him, ideals for a still distant future. Because of his family's prominence he had possessed rather easy access to positions that carried prestige, if not much exercise of originality, under the Viceroyalty. In his letters he speaks of how he had been a *regidor* or councilman, a syndic, a solicitor general, an alcalde, a member of the Consulate, and the Commander of the patriot regiment of Patricios.[2] Having rubbed shoulders with the governing class of Spaniards in the old days, he still cherished his special privileges. While later, after the panic of Huaqui, he would render valiant service to the patriot cause with his efforts to reorganize the routed army, in 1810 he felt that Moreno was pushing his reforms too fast.

Saavedra found a willing ear in Funes, although it is probable that the Dean, more ambitious and less naive than Saavedra, was the one to seek out the President first. Funes had hoped to dazzle Buenos Aires with his brilliance. He found, instead, that it was Moreno's articles which were on everybody's tongue.

The Dean spent many evenings in Saavedra's house planning how to undermine Moreno's influence. It was spring and the days were already warm. While the golden-blossomed acacia trees were beginning to bloom, an air of expectancy filled the capital. Clothed in his long, priest's robe, his face sharp and crafty in his conical hat, Dean Funes felt the expectancy and also felt the beginning November heat. Thus the shade of the corridor bordering the patio of Saavedra's house was especially gratifying to him as he talked to the Colonel, stiffly correct in his uniform with its bright blue coat adorned with gold braid.

The two men walk back and forth, discussing Moreno's articles on the goals of the Congress. Neither Funes nor Saavedra is pleased with suggestions for a government of checks and balances.

What can they do? Their discussions center on the fact that as matters now stand Moreno is the dominant figure of the present Junta of nine members. But with the nine provincial deputies who are now in Buenos Aires added to the Junta instead of to a Congress things could change.

"I can persuade those deputies to oppose him," Funes points out to Saavedra. "With nine more members of the Junta pledged beforehand to vote against his measures, he will no longer be able to guide the revolution! *Que le parece?*"

Saavedra holds his index finger pressed against the side of his long nose in caution. "*Cuidado!* He can turn everything the other way in the *Gaceta*. The people swallow it whole."

"Not necessarily." Narrowing his eyes, Funes thinks for a moment. "Don't be so sure. There's bound to be a way around those articles. Look. Why don't we propose a rule that all discussions within the new Junta on the objectives of the Congress be kept secret?"

"How can that help?"

"*No ves, amigo?* In that way Moreno can no longer explain them in the *Gaceta*. If he does the people will support him, demanding that we call a Congress and draw up a constitution. Then we are lost. No! We will keep our discussions secret." He grows ecstatic. "We will pass a rule!"

"If we can." The Colonel is skeptical.

Meanwhile, rumors are coming to Saavedra of how Moreno makes jokes at times on the pleasure Saavedra derives from using the Viceroy's coach and escort. It is true that Moreno did jest among his friends about these things.[3] He could not resist a sarcastic barb. As we have seen, bristling irony runs all through his articles on Abascal's and Casa Irujo's proclamations. And doubtless it struck him as satirical, too, that Saavedra should put so much emphasis on the old Viceregal trappings in the town that was struggling against such odds to throw off the old corrupt ways and make for itself new and better ones.

It was at this time, also, that Moreno was publishing in the *Gaceta* a Spanish translation of Rousseau's *Social Contract*. His prologue to this work, with its encouragement to the individual to read good authors and inform himself about his political rights, was in particular distasteful to Dean Funes, who was planning to work for the restitution of the Jesuits—an order which had done so much in the past towards forbidding the reading of just such authors as Rousseau. In his prologue, Moreno says:

In vain will be their intentions (intentions of the leaders of a great cause) and their...efforts...for the public welfare, in vain will they call congresses...and attack the relics of despotism, if the peoples themselves do not try to become better informed, if they do not popularize their rights, if each man does not know what he is worth, what he can be and what he ought to be. (If he does not do this), new illusions will follow the old ones, and after vacillating in a thousand incertitudes, it will be our fate, perhaps, only to have changed tyrants, without destroying tyranny.

In such critical circumstances, each citizen is obliged to communicate his knowledge; and the soldier who exposes his breast to the enemy does not perform a greater service than the learned man who abandons his ivory tower and attacks...ambition, ignorance, egoism and the other passions...which carry on a secret war...against the state..... I flatter myself that I have not viewed with indifference so sacred an obligation, from which no citizen is excepted. In this matter I would rather have merited the censure of being too bold, than that of being...indifferent.... But my knowledge being inferior to my zeal, I have found no other means of satisfying the latter than to reprint certain books on politics that have always been regarded as the catechism of free peoples.... Among the various works which ought to form this precious gift that I offer my fellow citizens, I have given first place to the *Social Contract*.[4]

Moreno went on to say that, since Rousseau had gone a little astray on religious matters, he would suppress the chapter and the passages which dealt with these. (It is interesting to note that a month after Moreno left the government, all the copies of the *Social Contract* which had been distributed were ordered to be turned in, as having been harmful to the youth of the country.) [5]

At the time of publication there was also talk about Moreno's overzealous daring in publishing this work. Yet his own articles on the purpose of the Congress were scarcely less daring. This daring and this impatience at the slow march of the people toward independence were, we are told, Moreno's chief faults. "Moreno's incurable impatience always caused him a struggle," Ricardo Levene says. "And the slow march of events before the vertigo of his thought provoked in him an extreme anguish."

We see this impatience still under control in his first articles on the Congress. In the *Gacetas* of November 6 and 13, he wrote:

> It is just that people expect everything good from their worthy representatives; but also it is fitting that they learn for themselves what is due their interests and rights. Happily it is observed among our peoples that, shaking off their ancient torpor, they manifest a noble spirit disposed for great things and capable of any sacrifice that leads to the consolidation of the general good.[6]

> The Laws of the Indies were not made for a nation, and already we are forming one. The supreme power that is erected must treat with other powers.... He who takes the place, by election of the Congress, of the person of the King who is prevented from ruling us, has no rules to guide him and it is necessary to predetermine them.... He must not be a despot and for this reason a well-regulated   constitution is imperative. We feel then...that the Congress has been called to erect a supreme authority which will supply the lack of the Señor Don Ferdinand VII, and to arrange a constitution.[7]

Even these logical and well-tempered thoughts caused a few heated discussions. No one had said openly, before, that the Congress would erect an authority to "supply the lack" of the King. Although this was understood among the intelligent patriots, it was considered a bold stroke to print the idea for everyone to read, and for those who could not read to hear from the priests who so often read the *Gaceta* after mass.

Doubtless, Funes suggested to Saavedra that this consternation among some of the people could and should be used against Moreno. For one thing, with a little prodding it could stimulate the deputies to demand that they enter the Junta as co-members, rather than as part of the Congress. The Congress, according to Dean Funes, looked like a touchy business. Perhaps it was better to postpone it. The old disease of the politician, relaxing into the path of least resistance, ceding to petty pressure rather than stepping out to lead boldly, this disease was thus strong even among these new politicians.

It must be remembered, however, that Funes, on the other hand, was not a new but an old hand at this sort of thing. He had been playing himself up in Córdoba for a long time. And Saavedra had been fuming impatiently in the Junta, visiting his old barracks from time to time, renewing his acquaintance with the men of his regiment where he was much more at ease than he was in the field of government. Both Saavedra and Funes pointed out to the deputies how much more comfortable and outstanding a position they would occupy as part of the already established Junta. Echoes of this kind of talk came to Moreno.

Yet in the circular he had directed to the Cabildos who were to elect deputies he had clearly indicated that they should come to discuss a new form of government. In none of the circulars sent out after the first quick note of May 27 had he mentioned incorporation in the Junta. Instead he had empahsized that these men should come to Buenos Aires prepared to discuss in a Congress the betterment of their provinces.

To Montevideo he had written:

A unity of aims among the towns can alone save

them from the dangers which threaten so near. One ven-
tures nothing in awaiting the results of a Congress in
which all should take part and where the true direction
fitting these provinces should be fixed.[8]

To the Cabildo of San Luis he had written:

> The elected deputy should leave immediately for this
> city and you should give him instructions on how to
> stimulate your population and commerce, leading it to
> the high grade of prosperity which the Junta desires for
> all the peoples of its command.[9]

In acknowledging the receipt of notes from Salta,
Tucumán, and Santiago del Estero which told of the nomination of their deputies, he wrote:

> The Junta is informed of the recognition this city
> has given it, and of the promptitude with which it has
> acted for remission of the deputy who is to come to the
> General Congress.[10]

Echoes of talk about how the deputies should enter the
Junta and postpone the Congress seemed unreal to Moreno.
Still he knew that lies were being spread against him by
agents of the counterrevolutionists. He had exposed in
former *Gacetas* the lies which the Viceroy of Peru had
spread about the Junta, as well as about the fortunes of
Spain in her fight against Napoleon. On November 8 he
wrote:

> We have received the copy of another proclamation
> published by Abascal. We will not detain ourselves to
> answer it. . . . Only we will make an observation on the
> historical part. . . . It is stated that at the moment our
> troops withdrew, conquered, from Buenos Aires, the
> troops of Córdoba passed over to us and that by means
> of this treason we, the insurgents, were able to take the
> person of Liniers, the Bishop, etc. Those who have
> witnessed the facts and know from the evidence what
> truly happened, will not be able to countenance such
> gross lies, lies which are proposed by these men as the

only basis for directing, at their whim, the opinion of all the people. . . . Unfortunate citizen of Lima who doubts the stupid accounts of Abascal, and unfortunate inhabitant of Montevideo who does not believe that in Buenos Aires there run rivers of blood, that there is no safety of person or property, that fires are made with doors and street posts, and that the generous subscription of the English merchants in favor of the Library has been a simulated subsidy to alleviate the scarcity and crisis of the treasury! Our enemies are nourished with these dreams. . .and we, firm in our sacred cause, march with straight and majestic step towards its perfection.[11]

Whether Moreno knew that even in Buenos Aires other lies were being circulated, this time about him personally, is not certain. Whatever the false accusations were, now that the populace was beginning to divide secretly into Saavedristas and Morenistas, he paid them little heed.[12] What he *did* do was to emphasize more fully in the *Gaceta* that the deputies had come to form a Constitutional Congress and that the Junta was provisional.[13]

He began to explain to the people how they had the same right to form a Congress as the people in Spain had to erect Juntas of self-government when the King was made captive.[14] But, he said:

The dissolution of the *Junta Central* (in Spain) restored to the towns the plenitude of their powers which no one except they themselves could exercise since the captivity of the King. . .loosened the chains which constituted him center and head of the social body. . . . But the Americas are not united to the Spanish monarchs even by the Social Pact, which alone can sustain the legitimacy. . .of a domination. . . . Force and violence were the only bases of the conquest which added these regions to the Spanish throne, a conquest which in 300 years has not been able to erase from the memory of man the atrocities and horrors with which it was executed. . . . Now, then, force does not induce right, nor can there be born from it a legitimate obligation to prevent us from resisting it.[15]

This began to look as if Moreno meant Buenos Aires to fight against forces headed by Ferdinand, if such an event should occur. There were doubtless some murmurs about this, but Moreno went on to say:

> I have indicated these principles because no right of the peoples ought to be hidden. . . . Would the King pretend that we should continue under our old constitution? We would reply to him justly that we know none, and that the arbitrary laws dictated by greed for slaves and colonists cannot regulate the fate of men who wish to be free and whom no power on earth can deprive of that right. Would the king aspire that we live in misery as before, and that we continue forming a group of men to whom a viceroy can say with impunity that they have been destined by nature to vegetate in obscurity and depression? Two million men would reply to him in a body: 'Imprudent man! What do you discover in your person which makes you superior to us? What would your Empire be if we hadn't given it to you? . . . . And if you wish to show yourself worthy of the elevated dignity we have conferred on you, you should be glad to see yourself placed at the head of a free nation, which in the firmness of its constitution presents an obstacle to the possible corruption of your sons, so that the land cannot be thrown into the disorders which, to your and the kingdom's ruin, dishonored the government of your parents.'
>
> Here are the just accusations which our present monarch would suffer if he should resist the constitution which the national Congress is to establish. They are derived from the essential obligations of society, born immediately from the social pact.[16]

These were strong words, stronger than he had used before. Some people were shocked by his imaginary address to King Ferdinand, beginning with the words "imprudent man!'' and emphasizing the fact that the King's powers had been "deposited" in him by the people and not by God, and that the people who had deposited them could therefore also take them away, in fact were obliged to do so if the King opposed a constitution for their welfare. In spite of the Encyclopedists and the new philosophy of individualism, the idea of the divine right of kings had not wholly disappeared. Moreno followed this address to the King by saying,

> In the just honor of a Prince who in the few instants he remained on the throne did not show any desire other than that of the welfare of his people, we ought to know that far from being aggravated by the wise constitution of our Congress, he will feel the greatest pleasure. . . . [17]

In spite of this mollifying appendage, the Secretary had said, in the open, words that no colonial government had dared utter before.

The creole youth were delighted. This was completely in line with their feeling of independence, with that exalted urge which Ignacio Nuñez, who was one of them, tells us he had felt from the beginning in his longing to go as far as Peru and start a revolution there. "So great was the delirium caused in us by the word 'Liberty' which sounded in our ears for the first time."[18] But many older people, jurists and theologians nourished on scholastic reasoning, resented the Secretary's new, bold way of speaking. He would speak later of "balancing the powers" in the new government, in order to put a check on any one man or department becoming too arbitrary. They would have preferred him to quote fewer ideas from Rousseau and Montesquieu and Jefferson and more from St. Thomas and St. Augustine.

Some people were confused, too, by his speaking of the King's countenancing a free constitution. Did Moreno mean that they should be free and still have the King? Alberti

cites certain passages of these articles later to prove that
Moreno was a monarchist. But aside from the fact that the
passages cited do not prove this allegation, we can only
agree with others, such as the historian Ricardo Levene,
that Moreno spoke out more forcibly in 1810 for independence and democratic institutions than anyone else. We
must remember also that he was speaking at a time when
the people could be persuaded more easily to set up the kind
of democratic government that existed in the constitutional
monarchy of England (which would flower still more fully in
the English dominions), thus keeping the King, than they
could be argued into an out-and-out republic without the
King. What Moreno was interested in was a democratic
government of the people in the most feasible way obtain-
able: either with the figurehead of the King or without it. In
any case, he was primarily a democrat, and it is only the
lesser men who came after him and wished to cull for themselves some of the honor of originating the ideas of democracy in La Plata who dispute his supreme contribution in
this field.

Levene has said:

> His mentality was a combination. He knew the
> French Encyclopedists and philosophers, but he had also
> been formed in the reading of jurists and historians of
> the Indies; the revolutionary wave led him to radical in-
> novation, but his observations of the atmosphere,
> customs and men restrained him. . . . Moreno had con-
> templated the process of development of liberal reforms
> adopted by Carlos III and Carlos IV, establishing the in-
> stitutions of the Viceroyalty and a progressive and new
> legislation without brusk alterations. The current of
> revolutionary ideas, which had been obscurely fed by the
> liberal plans of the Bourbons, began to move the
> viceregal organization and for four years had shaken it.
> The plan of a schematic constitution, like Moreno pro-
> posed, had, as object, the continuation of the Revolution

in an orderly manner, the opening of canals to the new forces engendered so as to prevent for the present the waters leaving the mother.[19]

Actually, what Moreno chiefly wanted was to get his articles read, and if he had started out by completely dispensing with the King, it is fairly certain they would have been burned. As it was, there was disagreement enough about his boldness.

Encouraged by the talk against him, the Spaniards aspiring to government posts started weaving a network of intrigue. They still expected help from outside, either from Lima or Montevideo. In the cafés and pulperías—those all-purpose corner grocery stores—Moreno's friends listened with dismay at what these men, after a little too much wine or rum, boasted they would do. Here and there a gaucho would challenge them and a duel with knives would take place, either on the street or in and out between the crowded tables, sacks of yerba maté and barrels of rum that lined the walls of the stores.

During the first week of December, when the weather became oppressively hot, the rumors flew more thickly and insolence flared. Moreno knew what to do about this. He had brought order after the attack on Judge Caspe, and he would bring it again. Besides, he was saturated with the bragging and plotting of the peninsular Spaniards. On December 3 he issued a decree which stated that no civil, ecclesiastic or military office could be held henceforth except by people born in the colonies, with the exception of those Europeans already in office, who should realize that their good conduct, love for the country and adhesion to the government would be a sure guarantee of their continuance in office and promotion. He stated that the reason for this change in the Junta's procedure was the "fatal disillusionment the Junta has received from men ungrateful to the country in which they have made their fortune, and also because of the principle that in no country is the government shared with foreigners.'' [20]

In order to show that this decree was aimed principally at the former ruling class of Spaniards, Moreno added a paragraph inviting foreigners to settle in the country and dedicate themselves to the arts and cultivation of the fields.

The decree accentuated the division in the city between Saavedristas and Morenistas. Almost every day since the revolution certain Spaniards had been obliged by the Junta to leave, starting with the former Viceroy, Cisneros, then the judges, and later on the members of the Cabildo. Saavedra, in the instructions written to his lawyer in 1814, said that he had opposed this system of exile. After the December 3 decree he doubtless gave vocal expression to sympathy with the people offended. As usual the youthful revolutionaries were on Moreno's side, however, except for the military clique, which Saavedra more or less controlled. It would not be long until the President made use of this advantage.

While the decree confining public office to men born in the country was being discussed, there were other plans going on in the patriot barracks of Patricios. These plans centered on preparations for a banquet and ball for the purpose of celebrating the victory of Suipacha. The idea was kept rather closely within military circles. When the time came for the celebration to be given in the barracks, orders were relayed to the sentinels who would guard the doors to allow free entrance only to men in uniform.

Meanwhile, Moreno, oblivious to the plans for the banquet, was busy writing his articles *On The Mission of The Congress*. While the general lines of strategy for the victory of Suipacha had been his, he was more interested in going forward than in detaining himself with elaborate celebrations to commemorate the victory. Besides, there were so many other enemy forces still to be met, so much to plan—a whole constitution to be drawn up.

Echoes of the talk about the deputies entering the Junta immediately, thus postponing the Congress, caused him to write at this time in the *Gaceta*:

> Even those who confuse sovereignty with the person of the monarch ought to be convinced that the reunion of the towns cannot have the small object of naming governors, without the establishment of a constitution whereby they are ruled.... The authority of the monarch returned to the peoples through the captivity of the King; they can then modify it, or subject it to the form which pleases them most, in the act of giving it over to a new representative.... The absolute ignorance of public right in which we have lived has caused equivocal ideas about the sublime principles of government, and things being judged by their brilliance, the sovereign of a nation has been generally believed to be he who governed it at his whim.... The true sovereignty of a people has never consisted in anything but the general will of the same; that sovereignty, being indivisible and inalienable, has never been able to be the property of one man alone... and while the governed do not have the character of a group of slaves or a sheepcote of sheep, the governors can be of no other type than that of executors and ministers of the laws which the general will has established.[21]

With this statement Moreno again exploded the idea of an absolute ruler on the pattern of the Viceroys or of a permanent Junta. But he also wanted to show the reasons for the temporary establishment of the present Junta and point out the difference between its emergency rule and the kind of representative government for all the provinces that was to come. He wrote:

> Buenos Aires should not erect by itself alone an

authority over towns which have not concurred with
their suffrage to its installation. The imminent danger
of delay, and the urgency with which nature excites men
to execute, each one for his part, what ought to be the
simultaneous work of all, legalized the formation of a
government to exercise the rights which had spon-
taneously returned to the people, and which it was
necessary to deposit promptly in order to prevent the
horrors of confusion and anarchy. But this people,
always great, always generous, always just in its
relationships, did not wish to usurp from the smallest
village the part that it should have in the erection of the
new government. It did not take advantage of the ascen-
dancy which the relationship of the Capital gave it over
the provinces; and establishing the Junta, it imposed
upon it the quality of provisional, limiting its duration to
the date for celebration of the Congress, and charging
the Congress with the installation of a firm government;
so that it would be a work of all those whom it equally
concerned. . . . This has been an act of justice of which
the capitals of Spain did not give us an example. . . . [22]

Should the Congress attempt to form a government for
all Spanish America? Moreno thought such an attempt
would be impossible at the time. He had no such ambitions
or grandiose views and here we find his statements quite
different from the viewpoint of the bloody "Plan of Government" later attributed to him. Yet it is interesting to note
that in one of his articles he went into the principles governing a Federal Union, quoting from Thomas Jefferson's
Notes on Virginia. Speaking of the federal government, he
wrote:

The great principle of this type of government is
that individual states, retaining the part of sovereignty
which they need for their internal affairs, cede to a
supreme and national authority the part of sovereignty
which we will call imminent for general business. . . .
This system is perhaps the best which has been dis-

air fragrant with perfume from rose bushes and the flowering trees. From time to time their guide flashes his light on the jutting iron-grilled balconies ahead of them, showing his masters how to keep in their path.

In spite of the beauty of the night Moreno is discouraged and tired. For the past month he has been troubled with indigestion. It is apparent that his intensive work, in the face of growing threats, has begun to take its toll. Already, mindful of the anonymous papers being circulated against him, his mother and his wife, Maria, have begun to plead with him to be more careful. It is true, he thinks, that recently agents from the royalists in Montevideo had slipped in on little boats at the hidden inlets. Even now they may have distributed early versions of the barbarous "Plan of Government" later attributed to him and to which they forged his signature. In places they had pasted up the *pasquines* which called him a "Jacobin" and a "demon," handbills that were quickly torn down by his indignant followers. But Moreno isn't thinking of his personal safety as he walks through the night with Larrea and with Tomás Guido, who has joined them.

His discouragement stems not from the threats against him but from the fact that he has not been able to stimulate more quickly the public spirit which he'd hoped to encourage in the people. The streets, for instance, which he had ordered to be repaired, are still pockmarked with holes and ditches. As they walk along he points out these places to his friends.

Now they are at the barracks. The noise of laughter and drinking from within float out the windows. Larrea stops the sentinel guarding the heavy portal and asks the man to let them enter. The sentinel shakes his head. This is an exclusive affair, he says. Only the military. No one else may be admitted.[26]

The poor man, Larrea decides, has not recognized who they are. He tells him to go call the Corporal of the Guard.

"No, no!" Moreno, an ironical smile on his lips, protests. "Haven't you seen, *compañero*? Is it for this kind of thing that we've been working?" [26] He cannot stomach the attitude of vainglorious militarism which the sentinel's words seem to convey.

Immediately he turns on his heels and, followed by his two friends, starts home.

Could it be that the sentinel *had* recognized the Secretary and felt it best for him not to witness the scene now taking place inside the barracks?

The last course of the banquet is being served. A huge cake is placed in front of the Saavedras, and on it lies a laurel wreath crown. Excitement ripples through the circle of men huddled together who are in on the scheme. Their hour has come.

"Go ahead, Duarte!" One of the soldiers pushes Atanasio Duarte forward.

The slightly drunken Sergeant walks up to the Saavedras. With a flourish he lifts one of the crowns of laurel leaves and presents it to the Señora de Saavedra. The Señora hands the crown to her husband. Then in a kind of heady delirium, Duarte raises his glass.

"To the Emperor Saavedra!" he cries. "America awaits with impatience the day — the day he shall take the scepter and the crown!"

An embarrassed laughter follows. Here and there can be heard scattered clapping. But chiefly there is embarrassment, both at the way Duarte totters and at the smile of satisfaction on the Saavedras' faces.

This proposal of an emperor for America is too much even for the military to take. They had not liked, for the most part, Moreno's strict rules about promotion based on merit, and compulsory education in the *School of Mathematics* before becoming an officer. But their opposition could not go so far as to make Saavedra or anyone else an Emperor. Duarte's schemers have overstepped themselves. At heart, even the soldiers want a republic someday, although most of them might have said, "It won't come in our lifetime."

All the same, the banquet proceeds in a gay mood, everyone trying to laugh off the incident as the whim of a slightly tipsy officer of the old school. Not so the ardent members of the former *Club of the Seven*, some of whom were there.

Later on that evening, Nicolas Rodríguez Peña and Antonio Beruitti come by Moreno's house and tell him of this insult to the *Patria*.[27]

Moreno's eyes blaze. He has become extremely thin. His face is pale and drawn.

"Incredible!" he exclaims. "Incredible."

"I assure you it happened," Nicolas says.

After the men have left he cannot sleep. He paces the floor of his study. God knows, he tells himself, he has not worked for this kind of thing. He has been trying to start a Congress that would draw up a democratic constitution, and now this ridiculous throwback, this demand for an Emperor, this foolish toast reminiscent of viceregal days of pomp and graft and irresponsibility. He is reminded of Liniers and his mistress and of Liniers' adoring letters to Napoleon. Suppose the royalists from Peru and Montevideo, hearing of Duarte's toast to Saavedra, should try to inflate it into counterrevolution from within the very heart of the city? Then they could call for aid from the Portuguese troops, already waiting on the border, anxious to put in Carlota. None of this must happen.

He sees what a mistake it has been to let Saavedra keep the trappings of the Viceroy. It is these things—the coach, the escort—which have confused the people and made possible this toast.

Some time during the night he wrote a decree for the suppression of the honors of the President. The next day he presented it to the Junta in a body to be voted on and it was approved. Even Saavedra did not protest. On the following day, December 8, the decree was circulated throughout the town in an extra issue of the *Gaceta*.[28]

If Funes, himself, had planned the incident of the toast and Moreno's reaction, he could not have planned better. The Dean rubbed his hands together in anticipation. This kind of thing, he told himself, would accentuate the division between Saavedristas and Morenistas. It could easily prepare the ground for his own domination later. Surely adherents of Moreno's most democratic principles would now start saying, "Of course we agree with his reasons, but couldn't he have waited until after the Congress? So soon after Duarte's joke of a toast, the decree is hard on Saavedra. Shouldn't Moreno have been more tactful?"

Yet the language of the decree was inspired, for it rang with an enthusiastic and genuine devotion to democracy. And it was logical. Moreno's words in the Junta meeting had carried the same ardent conviction. He usually persuaded everyone to his viewpoint, and this time apparently he had convinced, for the moment, even Saavedra.

In the decree he gave his reasons for abolishing all difference in escort and treatment between the President and other members of the Junta. The Junta as a whole was not distinguished much from the rest of the people, he said, and he wanted this to be true from now on of the President, too. About Saavedra his words were diplomatic, emphasizing how the President's modesty had been mortified.

But Moreno's belief in the Colonel's modesty was, of course, far too optimistic. The President was much more mortified after the decree than he had been before. Although he later said that he had consented to Moreno's circulation of the decree in order to turn the sympathy of the people toward himself, this is not likely. He doubtless fell under the spell of Mariano's logic in the Junta conference, and then later regretted it. Moreno must have forgotten human nature if he thought Saavedra would not, in the end, resent the order stripping him of the viceregal honors, as well as the decision to send Duarte, who had toasted him as Emperor, into exile.

The first opposition came from the soldiers. It was undoubtedly fanned by the adherents of Funes and Saavedra, who wished to incorporate the deputies from the provinces into the Junta and postpone the Congress. Quarrels and duels between Saavedristas and Morenistas multiplied in the cafés and pulperías. Anonymous *pasquines* against both Saavedra and Moreno appeared more openly. Someone remembered that some of the creoles in the 1809 revolt in Chuquisaca had met the fate of being decapitated by the Viceregal troops, and that later their heads had been exhibited on road posts as a warning. So one of the *pasquines* even announced that "Moreno's devil's head on a pike ought to be sent throughout the Viceroyalty." [29] Because of what had happened to the 1809 creoles, this threat contained a real element of danger and of reversion to the old system of terror.

Then one day came the warning to Maria. Not only a note, this time, but more. Attached to the paper saying she would soon be a widow was a mysterious package. Maria's hands shake uncontrollably as she picks up the thing which has been lanced into her lap as she sits sewing near her window to catch the light. She reads the note in horror. Then her eye catches sight of the black mourning fan and veil. She screams and drops them to the floor.[29]

Mesmerized with fear she can scarcely move. As she listens to the sounds outside—the receding footsteps of the messenger of the *pasquín*—her little boy rushes in to see what's the matter.

"*Que te pasa, Mamacita?*"

"*Nada, nada, chiquito.*" She tries to hide the note but he takes it from her and attempts to read it.

"It's against Papa, isn't it? That's crazy. Fray Cayetano says it is."

"I know, I know."

"Will Papa fight a duel now?" he asks, his pupils large with hero worship for his father, whom he is sure could fight a beautiful duel.

"Hush, child! Your father never fought a duel in his life. How can you?"

"But Mama. I'm a Morenista!" The child's eyes flash. "I shall fight a duel for father myself!"

Maria hugs the little boy to her.

"Besides, father killed Liniers in a duel!" the child goes on. "I know he did. That's what all the boys say."

"What lies!" Maria cries. "To think they repeat them. Even to you! Oh, my child!"

When he realizes Maria's fright Mariano feels a stab of conscience. How young she is after all—only 22. Ten years younger than himself.

"My love, my soul, forget it," he says. "All this will pass, Maria. You'll see."

"Mariano! Don't work late at the fort any more. Please!"

He begins to wish now that he had not gone so far in his opposition to Saavedra. When Maria asks him to revoke his decree, however, he does not heed her. Not even when someone provokes an incident against it in the patriot barracks. After all, he reasons, the people as a whole are in favor of the ruling. Although it's natural that the scattered incidents here and there against it should loom large, he tells Maria, in reality they represent a small group. He is sure he can control them. He has never dodged a challenge in his life, and he does not mean to dodge this one.

Nevertheless the barracks incident gave Funes and the deputies the excuse they were looking for to ask the Junta to call an extraordinary session, in which they would participate, to discuss their incorporation into the government. This session, they argued, was necessary in order to calm the agitation brought about by the December 6 decree. Their proposal for enlarging the Junta, giving it nine additional members, was a poor one. Instead of bringing decision and calm to the government, it would bring nothing but confusion. Moreno foresaw such an outcome and prepared to argue against it.

The session was called for December 18,[30] a time of year comparable in weather to July in the United States. Tempers were easily wrought up as the men came perspiring to the meeting. As usual they met in the Junta's hall of conferences in the old viceregal palace of the fort.

Dean Funes, with craftiness and art, holds the floor at first, speaking for incorporation to calm the recent disturbance. Moreno, already half ill, rises at once to answer him. He does not mince words. The way to calm the agitation, he says, is to take energetic measures. They had been taken before, after the attempt on Judge Caspe, for instance, and order had been restored. Besides, the agitation is confined to a few and can easily be controlled. Most people are for the decree.[20] But the main need is not to postpone the Congress, and the worst feature about incorporation of the deputies to govern immediately is that it would do this very thing.

Paso supports Moreno in this stand. But no one else in

the meeting appears to agree. Then both Paso and Moreno propose that the question be taken to the people to be voted on, since it is one that cannot be decided by the Junta alone. This proposal is promptly voted down.[31].

Sensing his advantage, Dean Funes rises to speak. He moves that incorporation of the deputies be put to a vote, and also that all meetings of the Junta from now on be secret. He realizes he cannot afford to let the public know that Moreno's ideas on the Congress would be postponed. Immediately this double resolution is seconded and the voting begins.

The strange feature of this arrangement is that the deputies—the interested party—are allowed to vote as well as the members of the Junta, the government already in power. Naturally with the deputies participating the cards are stacked for incorporation. As it turns out, however, the result may have been the same if only the Junta, by itself, had voted. Saavedra and Funes have prepared the ground well. Moreno's and Paso's votes are the only ones against the proposal for incorporation of the deputies into the Junta and against secret meetings as well as against postponement of the Congress. The others, saying that they know such procedure is contrary to law, explain that nevertheless they are voting for incorporation because of the emergency. It should be noted that Castelli and Belgrano, who might have voted with Moreno, were absent: Castelli in the north, and Belgrano on the borders of Paraguay.

Moreno's opponents had hoped to offset his dominance of the Junta, but had not contemplated losing him. His name held a kind of magic for the interior towns, with which he had been in constant correspondence. In these towns, it was Moreno who stood for liberty and for the improvement of the peoples' rights. Doubtless, both Funes and Saavedra would have liked to keep Moreno for the gruelling work of organization of government departments and direction of the expeditionary forces, for all that work in which he was so skilled, and which, until now, he had carried out with such vigor. Moreno, however, was not going to be used by these ambitious men. If democracy and the work of the Congress were to be postponed, then his services in the Junta, especially now that he had worked himself to the bone, must be at an end. He tendered his resignation immediately.

In resigning he said that he did so "because there having been pronounced in a singular way against" his person the discontent of those who started this discussion, his "permanence in the Junta could no longer be advantageous to the public service." [32]

"I carry the conviction that I have done my duty," he said, "and that error is on the side of those who persecute me. I do not regret the act of December 6, which has produced the present lack of faith in me. Rather I hope that some day I shall enjoy the gratitude of those who are now against me, but whom I pardon with all my heart, and whose erring conduct I view even with a certain kind of pleasure." And now he smiled in that winning way he had. "I prefer to the interest of my own credit that the people begin to think about their government, although they commit errors which they must later correct." [33]

Everyone begged Mariano to reconsider. They even implored him to stay on with the government. But he refused. Yet when some of the men pointed out that the absence of his name on circulars to the interior would cause a shock among the people and might even encourage a falling away from Buenos Aires, he consented to continue signing his name to the Junta's communications for the next few weeks. Such was his generosity.

He would not remain in Buenos Aires much longer. As soon as the meeting was over he took Saavedra aside and

asked him to send him on a mission to London to purchase
arms for the Junta's army. This was a mission which he,
himself, had been preparing for Hipolito Vieytes. The instructions he would carry included a stopover in Río de
Janeiro, where he was to persuade the foreign minister to
win over Carlota's approval of the Junta, so that she would
withdraw her troops from the border. In England he was to
contact the Marquis of Wellesley and ask for secret, if not
open, recognition of the Buenos Aires government, for
arms, and for two printing presses, as well as for British
pressure on Brazil not to be hostile.[34] Earlier, Moreno had
sent Irigoyen on a similar trip to England, which had failed
to secure arms, but which had inspired some favorable
publicity for the Junta in the London papers.

Whether Moreno asked for this mission, immediately
granted by Saavedra, or whether the mission was a scheme
to exile him, as has been suggested, no one can be sure. Certainly Mariano might well have worried lest his continued
presence in the city should bring more anxiety to Maria in
the form of the *pasquínes* and threats which had so terrified
her. Had he been allowed to institute the strong measures
he wanted he could have stopped these threats. As it was,
the voting down of his proposal together with the incorporation of the deputies into the Junta amounted, in reality,
to exile.

On January 24, 1811, accompanied by his brother,
Manuel, and young Tomás Guido, he prepares to embark on
a ship for London.[35]

Among the creoles who line the shore below the fortress to bid him farewell that day there are not many dry
eyes. The *hacendados* and the laborers of the fields, the
owners of small *quintas* and *ranchos* know that their
greatest friend is leaving. What will the government be
without him? Surely he would never leave unless there had

been some plot! How had it happened?

The young creoles of the *Club of the Seven*, the ardent patriots who form the vanguard of the true movement for independence, find it hard to keep their fingers from the hilts of their swords. They would have liked to rush on Moreno's opponents in the Junta. This, of course, is the last thing he would sanction. So they hold themselves in. Yet with the knowledge of his going they feel that something of their ideals, something of the spark of a true government of the people is waning and burning low among them. Why should he have to leave? He is the purest flame of their independence, the highest expression of their greatness.

Mariano feels the current of sympathy and urgency reaching out to him. What can he do to comfort them, to give them courage?

Paso is tugging at his arm. Brother Cayetano is wiping his sleeve across his eyes and his forehead. Maria's face is lifted up to his. His mother's arm is around Maria, and in his own arms his child moves restlessly, tightening his hold about his neck. Out there on the waves of *La Plata* his ship is waiting.

"I must give them a joke," Mariano tells himself. "I must think of something."

All at once his face lights up. The crowd of his admirers moves closer. His eyes flash.

"Yes, I am going away," Moreno laughs. "But don't think you will be rid of me entirely. . . . I'm going away, it's true. But look—the trail I leave behind me will be long!" [35]

The people laugh and weep by turns. Of course he has left his mark everywhere. True independence, freedom of trade and of the press, a government of the people. These mark his trail.

"Yes, Mariano, we shall pick up your trail!" Brother Cayetano cries.

"What do you mean, father?" his child asks. "What trail?"

"Don't you remember how Hansel and Gretel made a trail when they went into the forest?" Mariano whispers. "It was by this trail they found their way back, remember? I shall do the same as I leave you, *hijo mío*. Guard my trail well. By it, someday, I shall come back to you!"

At heart he was not nearly so confident of returning. Often to Manuel he had said, "I don't know what misfortune awaits me on this voyage."

As the ship progressed, his health began to fail rapidly. Everyday he felt weaker. The sea was extremely rough. From the beginning he had suffered from indigestion and acute restlessness, much as he had suffered as a youth on his way to Chuquisaca. Though he had begun to translate *The Voyage of the Young Anarcharsis* to send to his six-year-old son, he could not adjust himself to these days of comparative idleness.

Yet in all his misgivings about this trip even he had not realized how completely he had worn himself out. On the evening of the third of March, when his condition became much worse, the Captain gave him an overdose of emetic. On the next day, March 4, he lay dying in Manuel's arms.

He prayed to God to bless his innocent wife and child. Then he said, "Even though I die, may my *patria* live!" [36]

Moreno's body was lowered into the sea. Saavedra, upon hearing of the ocean burial, said in his funeral oration for the man whom he had forced into exile and whom all Buenos Aires mourned, "It took so much water to quench so much fire." [37]

The modern Argentine poet and artist, Cupertino del Campo, addressing Moreno in the last two stanzas of one of his poems, has said:

> *Tu corazón que era ascua y comburente*

y maza forjadora, en ese ambiente
de fragua golpeaba su latir.
Tanto fuego—no obstante le elocuente
exclamación de un prócer—ni la fuente
insondable del mar pudo extinguir.
Your heart—a live coal, a combustible
 molding hammer, in that atmosphere of the forge,
 struck again and again its ardent beat.
So much fire—notwithstanding the
 eloquent exclamation of another—not even the
 fathomless waters of the sea could extinguish.

So there passed, like a brief flash from the torch of liberty over the land of Buenos Aires, this vibrant young innovator, steeped in idealism and sacrifice, formed by the immense, free spaces of his native land, shaped by a gentle and saintly Franciscan friar, nourished on the Laws of the Indies and the old scholastic theology, and drawn up from their obscure and complex reasoning by the irresistible light of the new thought of Rousseau, Filangieri, Campomanes, Jovellanos, Adam Smith and Jefferson.

The anarchy produced in the enlarged Junta after Moreno's departure would have to await another great figure in order to push the revolution forward. Until the arrival of José de San Martín, about a year later, dictatorship ruled in Buenos Aires and the patriot army suffered many reverses. But the men Moreno had "formed" were still strong and resolved enough to give support to the great military leader whose cause his genius had made possible. Thanks to Mariano Moreno, Buenos Aires would finally become independent through the efforts of San Martín, who arrived on March 9, 1812, and in 1816 the Congress for which Moreno had worked so zealously would at last take place. It met, prophetically enough, in that town where he had fallen ill and recuperated so quickly on his way to Chu-

quisaca, the town lying in the foothills of the Andes called
Tucumán.

The *British Review*, in announcing Moreno's death,
called him "the Burke of South America."[38] In ideas, the
two men were upholders of justice and order. But Moreno,
with greater intensity, breathed and wrote and lived his
ideas. A creole among creoles, with a dignity that was his
heritage from Spanish forbears, he had dedicated himself to
forming his fellow patriots into "men." In so doing, he had
fulfilled the prophecy which Brother Cayetano, years ago,
had made for him.

Does his spirit yet live in the great Argentine nation today? The Franciscan, Cayetano, would have answered that
such a question was needless. Had not Mariano, himself,
with his usual sparkle and the bright flash of love for his
people burning in his glance, answered the question on the
day he left his native land? "I am going away, but the trail I
leave behind me will be long!"

Bibliography

Books

Angelis, Pedro de. *Colección de Obras y Documentos*. Buenos Aires: *Imprenta del Estado*, 1836.

Ambrosetti, Juan B. *Supersticiónes y Leyendas*. Buenos Aires: L. J. Rosso, 1884.

Aramburu, Julio. *Historia Argentina*. Vol. 1 & Il 8th Edition. Buenos Aires: *Libreria "del Colegio,"* 1960.

Bauzá, Francisco. *Dominación Española en el Uruguay*, 2d Edition. Montevideo: *Barreiro y Ramos*, 1895.

Bilbao, Manuel. *Buenos Aires desde su Fundación Hasta Nuestros Dias*. Buenos Aires: *Imprenta de Juan Alsina*, 1902.

Batolla, Q.C. *La Sociedad de Antaño*. Buenos Aires: Moloney y de Martino, 1908.

Bosch, Mariano G. *Teatro Antiguo de Buenos Aires*. Buenos Aires: *El Comercio*, 1904.

Calvo, D. Carlos. *Anales Históricos*. (5 Volumes.) Buenos Aires and Paris: A. Durand, 1864.

Calzadilla, Santiago. *Las Beldades de Mi Tiempo*. Buenos Aires: *Imprenta el Comercio*, 1919.

Capdevilla, Arturo. *Rivadavia y el Españolismo Liberal de La Revolución Argentina*. Buenos Aires: *El Ateneo*, 1931.

Carbia, Romulo D. *Historia Eclesiastica del Río de La Plata*. Buenos Aires: *Casa Editorial Alfa y Omega*, 1914.

Carbone, E. Oscar D. *El Patrimonio de San Martín* Buenos Aires: *Ministerio de Educacion y Justicia*, Serie II, No. XVI, *Museo Histórico Nacional*, 1960.

Chapman, Charles E. *A History of Spain*. New York: The Macmillan Co., 1931.

Chaves, Julio Cesar. *Castelli el Adalid de Mayo*. Buenos Aires: Ediciones Leviatan, 1957.

Colma, Alfredo. *La Revolución en La America Latina*. 2nd Edition. Buenos Aires: N. Gleizer, 1933.

Concolorcorvo. *El Lazarillo de Ciegos Caminantes*. Buenos Aires: *Imprenta de La Rovada*, 1773 and 1884.

Crow, John A. *The Epic of Latin America*. New York: Doubleday, 1946.

Cruz, Francisco. *Bases y Puntos de Partida para La Organización Política de La República Argentina*. Buenos Aires: *La Cultura Argentina*, 1915.

Daireaux, Godofredo. *Costumbres Criollos*. Buenos Aires: *Imprenta de La Nación*, 1915.

————. *Tipos Y Paisages*. Buenos Aires: *Prudent Hermanos y Moetzel*, 1901.

Del Campo, Cupertino. *Mensajes Liricos*. Buenos Aires: *El Bibliofilo*, 1937.

Echeverria, Esteban. *Obras Completas*, Vol. V. Buenos Aires: Zamorra, 1951.

Elordi, Guillermo F. *Mariano Moreno, Ciudadano Ilustre*. Buenos Aires: *El Ateneo*, 1943.

Frias, Dr. Bernardo. *Historia del General Güemes y de La Provincia de Salta o sea de La Independencia Argentina*, Vol. V. Buenos Aires: Romulo d'Uva, 1961.

Furlond, Guillermo. *La Revolución de Mayo*. 2nd Edition. Buenos Aires: Club de Lectores, 1960.

Galvan–Moreno, C. *Mariano Moreno*. 1st Edition. Buenos Aires: *Editorial Claridad*, 1960.

Gana, Alberto Blest. *Durante La Reconquista*, Vol. I & II, 4th Edition, Santiago de Chile: *Casa Editora Zig-Zag*, 1955.

Gandia, Enrique de. *Las Ideas Politicas de Mariano Moreno*. Buenos Aires: Peuser, S. A., 1946.

Garcia, Hijo, Juan Agustin. *La Ciudad Indiana*. Buenos Aires: *Angel Estrada & Cia.*, 1900.

Gonsalez–Arrili, Bernardo. *Hombres de Nuestra Tierra*. Buenos Aires: Kapelusz, 1948.

Groussac, Pablo. *Santiago de Liniers*. Buenos Aires: *Arnoldo Moen y Hermano, Editores*, 1907.

Guido, Tomás. *Los Sucesos de Mayo Contados por Sus Actores*. Buenos Aires: W. M. Jackson, Inc., 1907.

Guiraldes, Ricardo. *Don Segundo Sombra*. Madrid: Espasa–Calpe, 1930.

Gutierrez, Juan M., *Letras Argentinas*. Buenos Aires: El Ateneo, 1929.

Harrison, Margaret Hayne. *Captain of the Andes. (The Life of José de San Martín)*. New York: Richard Smith, 1943.

Hernandez, José. *El Gaucho Martín Fierro*. Buenos Aires: Coni, 1925.

Ingenieros, José. *La Evolución de Las Ideas Argentinas*. Buenos Aires: L. J. Rosso, 1918.

Jovellanos, G. M. de. *Obras Escogidas de Jovellanos, con Un Prologo de F. Soldevilla.* Paris: *Garnier Hermanos,* 1886.

Juan, Jorge y Ulloa, Antonio de. *A Voyage to South America, translated by John Adams.* London: Longman, 1813.

Las Casas, Bártolomé de. *Historia de Las Indias,* 4th Edition. Buenos Aires: *Libreria La Facultad,* 1926.

Leguizamon, Martiniano. *El Gaucho.* Buenos Aires: *Cia Sud Americana de Billetes de Banco,* 1916.

Levene, Ricardo. *Las Provincias Unidas del Sud en 1811.* Buenos Aires: *Imprenta de La Universidad,* 1940.

———. *La Revolución de Mayo y Mariano Moreno.* Buenos Aires: *Editorial Cientifica y Literaria Argentina, Atanasio Martinez,* 1925.

———. *Lecciónes de Historia Argentina.* Buenos Aires: *J. Lajouane & Cia,* 1928.

———. *Historia de Mariano Moreno.* Buenos Aires: Espassa–Calpe, 1945.

López, Lucio V. *La Gran Aldea.* Buenos Aires: Martin Biedma, 1884.

López, Vicente F. *Historia de La República Argentina,* 4th Edition (10 Volumes) Buenos Aires: *Libreria La Facultad,* 1926.

Lynch, Benito. *El Ingles de Los Guesos.* Madrid: Espasa–Calpe, 1926.

Martino, Julio Delfin. *Vida de Mariano Moreno.* Buenos Aires: *Talleres Signo Artes Graficas,* 1954.

Mitre, Bártolome. *Ensayos Historicos.* Buenos Aires: *La Cultura Argentina,* 1918.

———. *Historia de Belgrano y de La Independencia Argentina.* Buenos Aires: *Libreria La Facultad,* 1927.

Molina, Raul A. (Director). *Historia: Colección Mayo Patrocinada por La Comision Nacional de Homenaje al 150 Aniversario de La Revolución de Mayo 1810. (Vol. III, Belgrano. Vol. IV, Castelli. Vol. XVIII, Saavedra.)* Costa Rica: *Imprenta Sillares,* 1960.

Molinari, Diego Luis. *La Representación de Los Hacendados de Mariano Moreno: Su Ninguna Influencia en La Vida Económica del Pais y en Los Sucesos de Mayo de 1810.* Buenos Aires: *Universidad de Buenos Aires, Facultad de Ciencias Económicas,* 1939.

Morales, Ernesto. *Leyendas de Indias.* Buenos Aires: *El Ateneo,* 1928.

———. *Leyendas Guaraníes.* Buenos Aires: *El Ateneo,* 1929.

Moreno, Manuel. *Colección de Arengas en el Foro y Escritos del Dr. Don Mariano Moreno.* London: James Pickburn, 1836.

———. *Vida y Memorias del Dr. Don Mariano Moreno.* Buenos Aires: L. J. Rosso, 1937.

Nuñez, Ignacio. *Noticias Históricas de La República Argentina.* Buenos Aires:

O'Connor, Arturo Reynal. *Los Poetas Argentinos*. Buenos Aires: *Imprenta de José Tragant*, 1904.

Otero, Pacifico. *Estudio Biográfico sobre Fray Cayetano Rodríguez*. Cordoba, Argentina: *La Velocidad de F. Domenici*, 1899.

Outes, Felix F. *La Diplomacia de La Revolución*. Buenos Aires: Coni, 1911.

Palcos, Alberto. *Rivadavia, Ejecutor del Pensamiento de Mayo* (2 volumes.) La Plata, Argentina: *La Universidad de La Plata, Facultad de Humanidades y Sciencias de La Educación*, 1960.

Palma, Ricardo. *Tradiciones y Articulos Históricos*. Lima, Peru: *Imprenta Torres Aguirre*, 1899.

Pardo, Ramon Francisco. *Mariano Moreno*. (*Documentos I, Instituto Bonaerense de Numismatica y Antiguedades*). Buenos Aires: *Casa Pardo*, 1960.

Paz, Luis. *História General del Alto Peru, Hoy Bolivia*. Sucre, Bolivia: *Imprenta Bolívar*, 1919.

Piaggio, Monseñor Agustín. *Influencia del Clero en La Independencia Argentina*. Barcelona: Luis Gili, 1912.

Pillado, José Antonio. *Buenos Aires Colonial: Edificios y Costumbres*. Buenos Aires: *Cía Sud Americana de Billetes de Banco*, 1910.

Piñero, Norberto. *Escritos Politicos y Económicos de Mariano Moreno, Con Prologo de Norberto Pinero*. Buenos Aires: *La Cultura Argentina*, 1915.

Pueyrredón, Carlos. A. *En Tiempo de Los Virreyes*. Buenos Aires: L. J. Rosso, 1932.

Puiggros, Rodolfo. *El Pensamiento de Mariano Moreno*. Buenos Aires: *Editorial Lautaro*, 1942.

René-Moreno, Gabriel. *Los Ultimos Dias Coloniales del Alto Peru*. Santiago de Chile: Imprenta Cervantes, 1896.

Robertson, W. S. *History of the Latin American Nations*. New York: D. Appleton & Co., 1932.

_____. *Rise of the Spanish American Republics*. New York Appleton–Century Co. 1936.

Rojas, Ricardo. *Doctrina Democrática de Mariano Moreno, Con Noticia Preliminar por Ricardo Rojas*. Buenos Aires: *Libreria La Facultad de Juan Roldan*, 1915.

Ruiz–Guinazú, Enrique. *El Presidente Saavedra y El Pueblo Soberano de 1810*. First Edition. Buenos Aires: *Estrada Editores*, 1960.

_____. *Lord Strangford y La Revolución de Mayo*. Buenos Aires: *Libreria y Editorial La Facultad*, 1937.

Saguí, Francisco. *Los Ultimos Cuatro Años de La Dominacion Espanola en el Río de La Plata*. Buenos Aires: *Imprenta Americana*, 1874.

Sarmiento, Domingo F. *A Sarmiento Anthology* (*Translated from the*

Spanish by Stuart Edgar Grummon, edited, with introduction and notes by Allison Williams Bunkley.) Princeton: Princeton University Press, 1948.

_____. Facundo. Buenos Aires: L. J. Rosso, 1937.

_____. Recuerdos de Provincia. Buenos Aires: L. J. Rosso. 1937.

Trelles, Manuel Ricardo. Revista Patriotica del Pasado Argentino. Buenos Aires: Imprenta Europea, 1888.

Vigil, Carlos. Los Monumentos y Lugares Históricos de La Argentina. Buenos Aires: Editorial Atlantida, 1959.

Yaben, Jacinto. Biografias Argentinos y Sudamericanos, Vol. IV. Buenos Aires: Editorial Metropolis (Vols I through V), 1938–1940.

Ybarra, T. R. Bolivar, The Passionate Warrior. New York: Ives Washburn Inc., 1929.

Zimmerman, Saavedra A. Don Cornelio de Saavedra. Buenos Aires: Editorial J. Lajouane & Cia, Libreria Nacional, 1909.

Primary Sources

Buenos Aires, Argentina: National Archives, Department of History of the Faculty of Philosophy and Letters, University of Buenos Aires. Archives of Hacienda, File 131, of the year 1806, and File 133, of the year 1807, containing records of cases defended by Mariano Moreno.

Señora Maria Elena Williams Balcarce de Moreno (great granddaughter of Mariano Moreno.) Interview, December 14, 1961, at the Señora's home in Moron, Argentina.

Footnotes

Chapter I

Early Schooling in Buenos Aires

1. Ricardo Levene, *La Revolución de Mayo y Mariano Moreno* (1925) II, 307, note 2 (begun on 306). "Moreno had enemies...which explain the anonymous notes of lugubrious warnings directed against him in an epoch in which it was the custom to slander people in lampoons by an unknown author which circulated from house to house." (The words "Jacobin," "man of low sphere, plotting soul, and ugly words," and "demon of Hell" were used to describe Moreno by Saavedra in a letter written to Chiclana which Levene quotes on page 174 of Volume II of this work. It is probable such words were also used in the lampoons which, as was also the custom, were often attached to the sides of public buildings.)
2. Manuel Moreno, *Arengas en el Foro y Escritos del Dr. Don Mariano Moreno* (1836), *Prefacio*, CLX.
3. Ricardo Levene, *La .Revolución de Mayo y Mariano Moreno* (1925), II, 53.
4. Manuel Moreno, *Vida y Memorias del Dr. Don Mariano Moreno* (1937), 26.
5. Domingo Sarmiento, *Recuerdos de Provincia* (1937), 163.
6. Manuel Moreno, *Vida y Memorias del Dr. Don Mariano Moreno* (1937), 27.
5. Ibid. 28.
8. Vicente F. López, *Historia de La República Argentina* (1925), III, 131.
9. Manuel Moreno, *Vida y Memorias del Dr. Don Mariano Moreno* (1937), 34.
10. Ibid., 40.
11. Ibid., 40
12. Manuel Moreno, *Arengas en el Foro y Escritos del Dr. Don Mariano Moreno* (1836), *Prefacio*, XXXV.

13. Ricardo Levene, *La Revolución de Mayo y Mariano Moreno* (1925), III, 292.
14. Manuel Moreno, *Vida y Memorias del Dr. Don Mariano Moreno* (1937), 26.
15. Arturo Reynal O'Connor, *Los Poetas Argentinos* (1904), 357.
16. William Spence Robertson, *Rise of the Spanish Republics* (1936), 41.
17. Ricardo Levene, *Lecciones de Historia Argentina* (1928), I, 210.
18. Ibid., 231.
19. Ibid., 23.
20. Manuel Moreno, *Arengas en el Foro y Escritos del Dr. Don Mariano Moreno* (1836), *Prefacio*, XXI.
21. Enrique de Gandia, *Las Ideas Politicas de Mariano Moreno* (1946), 9.

Chapter II
Atmosphere of Town, Country and Family in Buenos Aires

1. Ricardo Levene, *Lecciónes de História Argentina* (1928), I, 372.
2. Jose Pillado, *Buenos Aires Colonial* (1920), 275.
3. Vicente F. López, *História de La República Argentina* (1926), 528, note.
4. Bártolomé Mitre, *História de Belgrano y de La Independencia Argentina* (1918), I, 82.
5. Ricardo Levene, *Lecciónes de Historia Argentina* (1928), I, 384.
6. Ricardo Levene, *La Revolución de Mayo y Mariano Moreno* (1925), I, 166.
7. Ibid., I, 165.
8. Manuel Moreno, *Vida y Memorias del Dr. Don Mariano Moreno* (1937), 23.
9. Ibid., 36.
10. Ibid., 25.
11. Ibid., 39.
12. Ibid., 39.
13. Arturo Reynal O'Connor, *Los Poetas Argentinos* (1904), 89.
14. José Ingenieros, *La Evolución de Las Ideas Argentinas* (1918), 152 (note.)
15. Vicente F. López, *História de La República Argentina* (1926), I, 510.

16. Manuel Moreno, *Arengas en el Foro y Escritos del Dr. Don Mariano Moreno, Prefacio,* CXXXII.
17. Vicente F. López, *História de la República Argentina,* I, 510.

Chapter III

Incident on the Road to Chuquisaca

1. Manuel Moreno, *Arengas en el Foro y Escritos del Dr. Don Mariano Moreno* (1836), *Prefacio,* XXIX.
2. Arturo Reynal O'Connor, *Los Poetas Argentinos* (1904), 304.
3. Ibid., 95.
4. Ibid., 306.
5. Manuel Moreno, *Aregas en el Foro y Escritos del Dr. Don Mariano Moreno* (1836), *Prefacio,* XXIV.
6. Ibid., *Prefacio,* XXVII.

Chapter IV

Legal Training, Career, and Romance in Chuquisaca

1. Manuel Moreno, *Arengas en el Foro y Escritos del Dr. Don. Mariano Moreno* (1836), *Prefacio,* XXXIII.
2. Manuel Moreno, *Vida y Memorias del Dr. Don Mariano Moreno* (1937), 47.
3. Gabriel René-Moreno, *Los Ultimos Días Coloniales del Alto Peru* (1896), 6–7.
4. Manuel Moreno, *Arengas en el Foro y Escritos del Dr. Don Mariano Moreno* (1836), *Prefacio,* XLI.
5. Ibid., *Prefacio,* XXXIV.
6. Ibid., *Prefacio,* XXXVII.
7. Manuel Moreno, *Vida y Memorias del Dr. Don Mariano Moreno* (1937), 57.

9. Ricardo Levene, *La Revolución de Mayo y Mariano Moreno* (1925), III, 22.
10. Ibid., III, 23. Moreno was encouraged to take this stand in support of the Indians by the example of an unusual judge, Victorian de Villava, who had recently pronounced a judgement in Chuquisaca against the exploitation of the *mitayos* which had been engaged in by the powerful and corrupt governor intendente of Potosí, Paula Sanz. In Levene's *História de Moreno* (1945), pages 37–38, we read that Villava's *Discurso Sobre La Mita* and *Apuntamientos Para La Reforma del Reino, Espana e Indias* were well known works of reform in 1802, at the time of his death and Moreno's dissertation.
11. Gabriel René–Moreno, *Los Ultimos Días Coloniales del Alto Peru* (1896), 6.
12. Luis Paz, *História General del Alto Peru, Hoy Bolivia* (1919), I, 203.
13. Ibid., I, 492.
14. Jacinto Yaben, *Biografías Argentinas y Sudamericanas* (1938–1940), IV, 21–22.
15. Luis Paz, *História General del Alto Peru, Hoy Bolivia* (1919), I, 202.
16. Ramon Francisco Pardo, *Mariano Moreno* (1960), 117.
17. The story of the gold buckles which Mariano's father considered his "decency," together with other family legends, was given to the author by the charming great granddaughter of Mariano Moreno, the Señora Maria Elena Williams Balcarce de Moreno, aged 97. The interview took place on December 14, 1961, at the Señora's home, Calle Mendoza 460, Moron, Argentina.
18. Ramon Francisco Pardo, *Mariano Moreno* (1960), 128.
19. Ibid., 130.
20. Manuel Moreno, *Arengas en el Foro y Escritos del Dr. Don Mariano Moreno* (1836), *Prefacio*, XXXIX.
21. Ramon Francisco Pardo, *Mariano Moreno* (1960), 130.

Chapter V

Lawyer in Buenos Aires During the English Invasions, 1806, 1807

1. Bernardo Gonsalez–Arrili, *Mariano Moreno* in the series, *Hombres de Nuestra Tierra* (1948), 36.

2. Manuel Moreno, Vida y Memorias del Dr. Don Mariano Moreno (1937), 72.

3. Ibid., 73.

4. Ibid., 82.

5. Ibid., 84.

6. Manuel Moreno, *Arengas en el Foro y Escritos del Dr. Don Mariano Moreno* (1836), *Prefacio*, XXXVI.

7. Ibid., *Prefacio*, XXXVII.

8. Ricardo Levene, *Lecciónes de Historia Argentina* (1928), I, 384.

9. Ibid., I, 386.

10. Richardo Levene, *La Revolución de Mayo y Mariano Moreno* (1925), I, 260.

11. Manuel Moreno, *Vida y Memorias del Dr. Don Mariano Moreno* (1937), 79.

12. Ricardo Levene, *Lecciónes de Historia Argentina* (1928), I, 387.

13. Ibid., I, 388.

14. Bártolomé Mitre, *História de Belgrano y de La Independencia Argentina* (1918), I, 126.

15. Ibid., I, 131.

16. Ibid., I, 136.

17. Ibid., I, 141.

18. Vicente F. López, *História de La República Argentina* (1926), II, 14.

19. Ibid., II, 16, 17.

20. Ibid., II, 21.

21. Manuel Moreno, *Arengas el el Foro y Escritos del Dr. Don Mariano Moreno* (1836), Prefacio, LXXVII.

22. Ibid., *Prefacio*, XCVII.

23. Ramon Francisco Pardo, *Mariano Moreno*, 41.

24. Manuel Moreno, *Arengas en el Foro y Escritos del Dr. Don Mariano Moreno* (1836), *Prefacio*, CIV.

25. Manuel Moreno, *Vida y Memorias del Dr. Don Mariano Moreno* (1937), 136.

26. Richardo Levene, *La Revolución de Mayo y Mariano Moreno* (1925), III, 27.

Chapter VI

Moreno's Cases in Defense of the Oppressed

1. Richardo Levene, *La Revolución de Mayo y Mariano Moreno* (1925), I, 78.

2. Vicente F. López, *História de La República Argentina* (1926), II, 216.
3. Pablo Groussac, *Santiago de Liniers* (1907), 196.
4. Vicente F. López, *História de La República Argentina* (1926), II, 225, 226.
5. Pablo Groussac, *Santiago de Liniers* (1907), 217.
6. Manuel Moreno, *Argenas en el Foro y Escritos del Dr. Don Mariano Moreno* (1836), *Prefacio*, CXX.
7. Ricardo Levene, *La Revolución de Mayo y Mariano Moreno* (1925), III, 59.
9. Ricardo Rojas, *Doctrina Democrática de Mariano Moreno* (1915), 267.
9. Pablo Groussac, *Santiago de Liniers* (1907), 278.
10. Bártolomé Mitre, *História de Belgrano y de La Independencia Argentina* (1918), I, 253.
11. Ricardo Levene, *La Revolución de Mayo y Mariano Moreno* (1925), I, 146, note 1 quotes Manuel Moreno as saying that Mariano demanded that Alzaga's proposed Junta include creoles.

Chapter VII

Moreno Defends Free Trade—Hints of Independence

1. Richardo Levene, *La Revolución de Mayo y Mariano Moreno* (1925), I, 76.
2. Manuel Moreno, *Arengas en el Foro y Escritos del Dr. Don Mariano Moreno* (1836), *Prefacio*, CXLVI.
3. Vicente F. López, *História de La República Argentina* (1926), III, 119.
4. Ibid., II, 298.
5. Ibid., II, 273.
6. Ibid., II, 330.
7. Ibid., II, 330–334.
8. Ibid., II, 318.
9. Ricardo Levene, *La Revolución de Mayo y Mariano Moreno* (1925), I, 206.
10. Ibid., I, 205.
11. Ibid., I, 214.
12. Ibid., I, 226.

13. Ibid., I, 165.
14. Manuel Moreno, *Arengas en el Foro y Escritos del Dr. Don Mariano Moreno, Prefacio*, CI.
15. Ricardo Rojas, *Doctrina Democrática de Mariano Moreno*, 64 (Reproduction of *La Representación de Los Hacendados*, 27–108).
16. Ibid., 65.
17. Ibid., 69.
18. Norberto Piñero, *Escritos Politicos y Económicos de Mariano Moreno*, 126 (Reproduction of *La Representación de Los Hacendados*, 112–179).
Ib. id., 132.

Chapter VIII

The Beginnings of Revolution

1. Manuel Moreno, *Arengas en el Foro y Escritos del Dr. Don Mariano Moreno* (1836), *Prefacio*, CIV.
2. Vicente F. López, *História de La República Argentina* (1926), II, 364.
3. Ibid., II, 368.
4. Ibid., II, 375.
5. Manuel Moreno, *Arengas en el Foro y Escritos del Dr. Don Mariano Moreno* (1836), *Prefacio*, CXXI.
6. Vicente F. López, *História de La República Argentina* (1926), III, 16.
7. Manuel Moreno, *Arengas en el Foro y Escritos del Dr. Don Mariano Moreno* (1836), *Prefacio*, CXXV.
8. Vicente F. López, *História* de La República Argentina (1926), III, 42.
9. Ibid., III, 42.
10. Tomás Guido, *Reseña Histórica* in *Los Sucesos de Mayo Contados por Sus Actores* (1907), 201.

Chapter IX

Moreno Becomes Secretary of Government and of War in the Revolutionary Junta of 1810

1. Manuel Moreno, *Arengas en el Foro y Escritos del Dr. Don Mariano Moreno* (1836), *Prefacio*, CXXXII.
2. Ibid., *Prefacio*, CXXXII.
3. Ricardo Levene, *La Revolución de Mayo y Mariano Moreno* (1925), II, 64, note (2).
5. Manuel Moreno, *Arengas en el Foro y Escritos del Dr. Don Mariano Moreno* (1836), *Prefacio*, CXXXVI.
6. Vicente F. López, *História de La República Argentina* (1926), III, 63.

Chapter X

**Control of Counterrevolution
Freedom of the Press**

1. Ricardo Levene, *La Revolución de Mayo y Mariano Moreno* (1925), II, 91.
2. Ibid., II, 93, note 2.
3. Ibid., II, 93.
4. Manuel Moreno, *Arengas en el Foro y Escritos del Dr. Don Mariano Moreno* (1836), *Prefacio*, CXL.
5. Ricardo Levene, *La Revolución de Mayo y Mariano Moreno* (1925), II, 94, note 1.
6. Ibid., II, 95.
7. Ibid., II, 95.
8. Ibid., II, 96.
9. Ricardo Rojas, *Doctrina Democrática de Mariano Moreno, Con Noticia Preliminar por Ricardo Rojas* (1915), 112.
10. Ibid., 112, 113.
11. Ibid., 118.
12. Ibid., 117.
13. Ricardo Levene, *La Revolución de Mayo y Mariano Moreno* 1925), II, 97, note. 2.

14. Ibid., II, 98.
15. Ibid., II, 99.
16. Ibid., II, 101.
17. Vicente F. López, *História de La República Argentina* (1926), III, 65.
18. Manuel Moreno, *Arengas en el Foro y Escritos del Dr. Don Mariano Moreno* (1836), *Prefacio*, CLII.
19. Pablo Groussac, *Santiago de Liniers* (1907), 371. What Groussac says is, "If in the end and against all odds independence was realized, and it is most just that posterity place in the Argentine Pantheon the glorious patriot (Mariano Moren) whose successes and merits more than covered his faults, still history cannot fail to point them out. . . ." Groussac refers here to Moreno's having kept the "mask of Ferdinand" when his aim and that of the Junta were complete independence from Ferdinand and Spain.

Chapter XI

Consolidation of Democratic Rule
Expedition to the Interior

(Most of the quoted passages from Moreno's official pronouncements and dispatches are duplicates of Ricardo Levene's paraphrased extracts from the National Archives of Argentina, and are thus cited below, with Levene as the source.)

1. Ricardo Levene, *La Revolución de Mayo y Mariano Moreno* (1925), II, 109.
2. Ibid., II, 109, note 1.
3. Pablo Groussac, *Santiago de Liniers* (1907), 388.
4. Ricardo Levene, *La Revolución de Mayo y Mariano Moreno* (1925), II, 87.
5. Ibid., II, 202, 207.
6. Ibid., II, 205.
7. Bártolomé Mitre, *História de Belgrano y de La Independencia Argentina* (1918), I, 330.
8. Ricardo Levene, *La Revolución de Mayo y Mariano Moreno* (1925), II, 211.

9. Ibid., II, 218.
10. Ibid., II, 133.
11. Ibid., II, 134.
12. Ibid., II, 134, Note (1).
13. Vicente F. López, *História de La República Argentina* (1926), III, 159.
14. Bártolomé Mitre, *História de Belgrano y de La Independencia Argentina* (1927), I, 168.
15. Ricardo Levene, *La Revolución de Mayo y Mariano Moreno* (1925), II, 138.
16. Vicente F. López, *História de La República Argentina* (1926), III, 160.
17. Ricardo Levene, *La Revolución de Mayo y Mariano Moreno* (1925), II, 139.
18. Ibid., II, 139.
19. Ibid., II, 117.
20. Ibid., II, 139.
21. Ibid., II, 117.
22. Ibid., II, 140.
23. Ibid., II, 140.

Chapter XII

Moreno's Guidance of the Auxiliary Expedition to the Interior—Repulse of Spanish Attempts at Blockade

1. Manuel Moreno, *Vida y Memorias del Dr. Don Mariano Moreno* (1937), 185.
2. Ricardo Levene, *La Revolución de Mayo y Mariano Moreno* (1925), II, 141.
3. Arturo Reynal O'Connor, *Los Poetas Argentinos* (1904), 357.
4. Ricardo Levene, *La Revolución de Mayo y Mariano Moreno* (1925), II, 145.
5. Ibid., II, 145.
6. Ibid., II, 147–148.
7. Ibid., II, 148, note 2.
8. Ibid., II, 153.
9. Ibid., II, 151.

10. Ibid., II, 153.
11. Ricardo Rojas, *Doctrina Democrática de Mariano Moreno, Con Noticia Preliminar por Ricardo Rojas* (1915), 123.
12. Ricardo Levene, *La Revolución de Mayo y Mariano Moreno* (1925), II, 134, note 3.
13. Ricardo Rojas, *Doctrina Democrática de Mariano Moreno, Con Noticia Preliminar por Ricardo Rojas* (1915), 124, 133.
14. Ricardo Levene, *La Revolución de Mayo y Mariano Moreno* (1925), II, 229.
15. Ricardo Rojas, *Doctrina Democrática de Mariano Moreno, Con Noticia Preliminar por Ricardo Rojas* (1915), 200, 201.
16. Ibid., 201.
17. Ibid., 183, 184.
18. Ibid., 181.
19. Ibid., 184–185.
20. Vicente F. López, *História de la República Argentina*, III, 226–229.
21. Ricardo Levene, *Lecciónes de Historia Argentina* (1928), I, 199.
22. Ricardo Rojas, *Doctrina Democrática de Mariano Moreno, Con Noticia Preliminar por Ricardo Rojas* (1915), 197–198.

Chapter XIII

Moreno's Plans for a Congress to Draw up a Constitution—Translation of Rousseau's Social Contract

1. Ricardo Levene, *La Revolución de Mayo y Mariano Moreno* (1925), II, 227.
2. Ibid., II, 227.
3. Ibid., II, 227.
4. Ibid., II, 226.
5. Ibid., II, 229, note 1.
6. Vicente F. López, *História de La República Argentina* (1926), III, 177.
7. Ricardo Levene, *La Revolución de Mayo y Mariano Moreno* (1925), III, 52.

8. Pablo Groussac, *Santiago de Liniers* (1907), 376.
9. Ricardo Levene, *La Revolución de Mayo y Mariano Moreno* (1925), II, 208.
10. Ibid., II, 210.
11. Ibid., II, 210.
12. Ibid., II, 208.
13. Ibid., II, 208, note 4.
14. Ibid., II, 208, note 4.
15. Ibid., II, 209.
16. Manuel Moreno, *Arengas en el Foro y Escritos del Dr. Don Mariano Moreno* (1836), *Prefacio*, CXL.
17. Ricardo Levene, *La Revolución de Mayo y Mariano Moreno* (1925), II, 290.
18. Manuel Moreno, *Arengas en el Foro y Escritos del Dr. Don Mariano Moreno* (1836), *Prefacio*, CLX.
19. Ibid., *Prefacio*, CLX.
20. Manuel Moreno, *Vida y Memorias del Dr. Don Mariano Moreno* (1937), 199.
21. Ibid., 199.
22. Ibid., 199.
23. Pablo Groussac, *Santiago de Liniers* (1907), 395.
24. Ricardo Levene, *La Revolución de Mayo y Mariano Moreno* (1925), II, 264.
25. Ibid., II, 263.
26. Ibid., II, 282.
27. Ibid., II, 149.
28. Ibid., II, 149, note (2).
29. Ibid., II, 153.
30. Vicente F. López, *História de La República Argentina* (1926), III, 194.
31. Ibid., III, 194–195, 197.
32. Ricardo Levene, *La Revolución de Mayo y Mariano Moreno*, II, 155
33. Ibid., II, 155.
34. Mariano Moreno, *Disertación Juridica Sobre el Servicio Personal de Los Indios* in *La Revolución de Mayo y Mariano Moreno* by Ricardo Levene (1925), III, 23.
35. Ricardo Levene, *La Revolución de Mayo y Mariano Moreno* (1925), II, 159.
36. Ibid., II, 154.
37. Ricardo Rojas *Doctrina Democrática de Mariano Moreno, Con Noticia Preliminar por Ricardo Rojas* (1915), 178–180.
38. Ricardo Levene, *La Revolución de Mayo y Mariano Moreno* (1925), II, 289.

Chapter XIV

Exile and Death

1. Ricardo Levene, *La Revolución de Mayo y Mariano Moreno* (1925), II, 292.
2. A. Saavedra Zimmerman, *Don Cornelio de Saavedra* (1909), 170.
3. Ignacio Nuñez, *Noticias Históricas de La República Argentina* (1857), 139.
4. Ricardo Rojas, *Doctrina Democrática de Mariano Moreno, Con Noticia Preliminar por Ricardo Rojas* (1915) 298.
5. Ricardo Levene, *La Revolución de Mayo y Mariano Moreno* (1925), II, 205.
6. Ibid., II, 264.
7. Norberto Piñero, *Escritos Politicos y Económicos de Mariano Moreno* (1915), 287.
8. Ricardo Levene, *La Revolución de Mayo y Mariano Moreno* (1925), II, 250.
9. Ibid., II, 250.
10. Ibid., II, 250.
11. Ricardo Rojas, *Doctrina Democrática de Mariano Moreno, Con Noticia Preliminar por Ricardo Rojas* (1915), 220, 221.
12. Norberto Piñero, *Escritos Politicos y Económicos de Mariano Moreno* (1915), 278–291, passim.
13. Ibid., 282, 292–293.
14. Ibid., 293.
15. Ibid., 278, 279, 290.
16. Ibid., 292, 293.
17. Ibid., 293.
18. Ignacio Nuñez, *Noticias Históricas de La República Argentina* (1857), 135.
19. Ricardo Levene, *La Revolución de Mayo y Mariano Moreno* (1925), II, 273.
20. Ibid., II, 288.
21. Norberto Piñero, *Escritos Politicos y Económicos de Mariano Moreno* (1915), 285.
22. Ibid., 282.
23. Ibid., 299–300.
24. Bernardo Gonsalez-Arrili, *Mariano Moreno*, in series, *Hombres de Nuestra Tierra* (1948), 89.
25. Vicente F. López, *História de La República Argentina*, III, 253–254.

26. Ibid., III, 254.
27. Ibid., III, 255.
28. Ibid., III, 257.
29. Ricardo Levene, *La Revolución de Mayo y Mariano Moreno* (1925), II, 307, note.
30. Ibid., II, 298.
31. Manuel Moreno, *Arengas en el Foro y Escritos del Dr. Don Mariano Moreno* (1836), *Prefacio*, CLXXV.
32. Ibid., *Prefacio*, CLXXV.
33. Ibid., *Prefacio*, CLXXVI.
34. Julio Delfin Martino, *La Vida de Mariano Moreno* (1954), 193.
35. Ricardo Levene, *La Revolución de Mayo y Mariano Moreno* (1925), II, 307.
36. Manuel Moreno, *Vida y Memorias del Dr. Don Mariano Moreno*, 241.
37. A. Saavedra Zimmerman, *Don Cornelio de Saavedra*, 83.
38. Ricardo Levene, *La Revolución de Mayo y Mariano Morenoz*, II, 307.